Robert Sommer teaches psychology and environmental studies at the University of California at Davis. He has been a Visiting Professor in the Departments of Architecture at the University of Washington and Berkeley. He is author of *Personal Space, Design Awareness,* and various articles dealing with the effects of buildings on people.

TIGHT SPACES

Hard Architecture
and How to Humanize It

ROBERT SOMMER

Prentice-Hall, Inc.  *Englewood Cliffs, N. J.*

A SPECTRUM BOOK

Library of Congress Cataloging in Publication Data

SOMMER, ROBERT.
  Tight spaces; hard architecture and how to humanize it.

  (A Spectrum Book)
  Includes bibliographical references.
  1. Architecture, Modern—20th century. 2. Architecture—Psychological aspects. 3. Architecture and society. I. Title.
  NA680.S65 1974   720'.1   73–21844
  ISBN 0–13–921346–5
  ISBN 0–13–921338–4 (pbk.)

NA680
S65
1974

10 9 8 7 6 5 4 3 2 1

PRENTICE–HALL INTERNATIONAL, INC. (LONDON)
PRENTICE–HALL OF AUSTRALIA, PTY. LTD. (SYDNEY)
PRENTICE–HALL OF CANADA, LTD. (TORONTO)
PRENTICE–HALL OF INDIA PRIVATE LIMITED (NEW DELHI)
PRENTICE–HALL OF JAPAN, INC. (TOKYO)

PREFACE

There is a massive effort today to gain security through steel, concrete, and electronic equipment. The prison has become the model for housing developments, commercial buildings, and even airports. It has been overlooked that the prison is not a very successful institution either in protecting society or in providing security for inmates or guards. Apart from an occasional lifer who is so adjusted to living in institutions that he cannot live outside, no one feels secure in prison. In the following chapters I will discuss the assumptions behind hard buildings, their effects upon occupants, and what can be done to humanize them. The last category is the most difficult to deal with. The obvious conclusion is that San Quentin, Pruitt-Igoe, and the Irvine Campus of the University of California should never have been constructed in the first place. The scale, scope, and impermeability of the architecture is oppressive to the human spirit. Build a university twenty miles from a city, arrange the offices and classrooms so that people can never meet, put the money into parking lots instead of lounges, develop an incentive system around individual achievement rather than common effort, and the result will be an alienating campus. The walled and fortified housing development, the instant campus, the security high school without exterior windows—all are inorganic and monumental. To identify similarities between institutions, for example between prison and zoo, does not mean that they are identical in purpose or conception, any more than it means that prisoners are animals. Confinement under oppressive conditions results in adaptations that are rarely in the best interests of the confined individuals or society.

Architecture as a profession began with the design of temples, altars, and great public buildings. Today the concern is still with public buildings, but these now include libraries, hospitals, post offices, and office buildings. Only a small percentage of private housing is architect-designed and even this amount is dwindling rapidly. The concern of the design professions has been and remains with the public environment. This is not to imply that designers have no role in residential building. Far from it, I believe that any designer could earn a per diem fee helping the occupants of a tract home or apartment to improve the quality of their living space. This kind of activity would be a healthy corrective to the present trend for architects to have little direct contact with the people who occupy buildings. Generally the architect is recruited by one group of people (clients), typically a corporate board or public agency, to design something for another group of people (consumers). The danger in such an arrangement is that the consumer becomes a faceless non-person.

Although this book is concerned with buildings and what can be done to humanize them, it is not intended solely for designers. Buildings should be everybody's business. It is a mistake to think of the built environment as the responsibility of a remote professional class. By themselves, architects, interior designers, and landscape designers lack the political power to realize their own ends. What gets built reflects more the values of banks and government agencies than designers. Architects in particular lack a political constituency for good design. The immediate task of the design professions is to awaken consciousness to the physical environment. Not every person need be a designer, but at least people can be put in touch with the spaces in which they live, work, and play. When the role that designers play in monumental buildings is discussed I do not imply that they are solely responsible. In a complex bureaucratized society nobody, except people who are so remote that they cannot be expected to know anything in particular, seems responsible for anything. The solution is tangible action on a local level by the people immediately concerned with a problem. The goal of this book is to raise public awareness about buildings and their effects. It may be a debatable instructional device to use the predicament of the caged zoo animal or prison inmate to accomplish this; however we will also discuss the airport terminal, the schoolhouse, and the office building.

The ideas expressed here owe much to Humphry Osmond, whose provocative letters sparked several chapters and to whom this book is dedicated. If geography had been more kind, this book would have undoubtedly been co-authored. I owe much to the ideas of Frank Becker, Philip Theil, Sim van der Ryn, and Murray Silverstein, and most of all to Barbara Sommer, for critically reading the chapters and Margaret Hill, who typed the manuscript.

Portions of this book that appeared in articles are used with the permission of the publisher—"What Do We Learn at the Zoo?" from *Natural History*, "The Security State of Mind" from *The Nation*, "The Lonely Airport Crowd" and "Waiting Rooms Versus Professor" from *Air Travel World*, and portions of "Symptoms of Institutional Care" from *Social Problems*. Some of the material on prison design came from a report prepared by the writer for the LEAA branch of the Department of Justice.

CONTENTS

Hard Architecture

Prison fixtures are being installed in the restrooms of city parks. According to the manufacturers' statements, they are supposed to be vandal-proof. One advertisement shows a man attacking a toilet with a sledgehammer. According to Sacramento, California Recreation Director Solon Wisham, Jr., "There is no exposed plumbing in the new buildings. The external fixtures are made of cast aluminum covered with hard epoxy. The buildings themselves are made of concrete blocks rather than wood or brick." [1] This same trend toward hard buildings is evident in public facilities across the country. Picnic tables are being cast of concrete rather than built of wood and are embedded several feet into the ground. It isn't possible to move these tables to a shady place or combine two tables to accommodate a large group, but that is an inconvenience for the users rather than the park officials. The older wood and metal tables remaining from a happier era are chained to blocks of concrete or steel posts.

The original inspiration for the park restroom, the prison cell, illustrates the hard facts of hard architecture. Human beings are enclosed in steel cages with the bare minimum of furnishings or amenities. In some cells there may be no furniture whatever except for the furthest advance in the field of vandal-proof plumbing, the hole in the concrete floor, otherwise known as a Chinese toilet. Because nothing is provided that the inmate might destroy, he may have to sleep on a bare concrete floor without mattress or blanket. I am not talking about the Middle Ages or some backward part of the nation. I have a clear image of an isolation cell circa 1973 with a man in a steel cage for 23 hours a day with nothing to do but pace the floor and curse the guard

---

[1] Jeff Raimundo, "Park Facilities are Still Vulnerable," Sacramento *Bee,* February 8, 1973, p. B1.

watching him through the slit in a steel door. The architecture of the isolation cell is based on a variant of Murphy's Law—if something can be destroyed, it will be destroyed.[2] In mental hospitals of the early 1950s, the line was, "If you give the patients anything nice, they won't take care of it." For public housing tenants it went "If you provide good architecture they won't appreciate it." There is the same denigrating we/they dichotomy in all these assessments of people's response to their surroundings. We know what's best for them and they don't. Even if we provide what they say they'd like, they won't take care of it and will probably destroy it. Ergo, it is best for everyone, especially the taxpayers who foot the bill, to design things that cannot be destroyed.

The result is that architecture is designed to be strong and resistant to human imprint. To the inhabitants it seems impervious, impersonal, and inorganic. Lady Allen, who pioneered the adventure playground in Great Britain, was appalled at American play yards which she described as "an administrator's heaven and a child's hell . . . asphalt barracks yards behind wire mesh screen barriers" built primarily for ease and economy of maintenance.[3] There is a whole industry built around supplying steel cages for prisons, wire mesh fences for city parks, and graffiti-resistant paint for public buildings. On a larger scale, the hardening of the landscape is evident in the ever-growing freeway system, the residential and second-home subdivisions pushing aside orchards and forests, the straightening and cementing of river beds, the walled and guarded cities of suburbia, and the TV cameras in banks and apartment buildings.

Another characteristic of hard architecture is a lack of permeability between inside and out. Often this means an absence of windows, a style referred to in Berkeley as post-revolutionary architecture. At first glance the Bank of America on Berkeley's Telegraph Avenue seems to have windows but these are really reflecting metal surfaces. The new postal center in Oakland, with its tiny slit windows, looks as if it were intended for urban guerilla warfare. Older buildings that still have plate glass use steel shutters and gates that can be drawn across the exterior in a matter of minutes. Some corporations are moving their

[2] Murphy's Law, No. 1: If something can go wrong, it will. Law No. 2: The toast always falls butter side down.

[3] Lady Allen of Hurtwood, *Planning for Play* (Cambridge: M.I.T. Press, 1968).

data-processing machinery underground where they are less vulnerable to attack. The fact that employees must work underground forty hours a week is a minor cost borne by the employees rather than the architect.

Hard architecture means wall surfaces that resist human imprint. Dark colors and rough cement were satisfactory prior to the advent of the aerosol can. The counter response of the hard-line designers has taken two forms. The first is the legal effort to remove aerosol cans from the hands of potential graffitists. Ordinances have been proposed to make it illegal to carry open aerosol cans on city streets. A New York State Senator has proposed a bill to make it illegal for people under eighteen to purchase cans of spray paint. The other approach is to develop vandal-resistant surfaces and stronger kinds of paint remover. In a six-month period New York City purchased 7,000 gallons of a yellow jelly called DWR (dirty word remover) from a Moorestown, N.J. manufacturer of industrial chemicals. The remover comes in two strengths and the heavier duty version is optimistically called Enzitall.[4] Planners of President Nixon's inauguration sprayed the trees alongside the motorcade route with a material that prevented birds from roosting there. They didn't want the president being embarrassed by an occasional bird-dropping. The two-year interval during which the birds would be unable to roost on these trees is a minor inconvenience again borne by the users.

Most of these efforts to harden the environment have had the avowed purpose of increasing security. Frequently this reason is a coverup for a desire to maintain order, discipline, or control. Although these motives are related to security, there are important differences between security and control that must be recognized and heeded if a democratic society is to continue. Let us examine the search for security that lies behind so much of the hardening process in public buildings and facilities.

THE SECURITY STATE OF MIND

Not too long ago, gas stations stopped accepting cash after ten in the evening. Then bus drivers stopped making change at any time. Taxi companies installed bullet-proof glass, and for the first time in history

---

[4] "Help Arrives," Cincinnati *Enquirer*, April 23, 1972.

New York cabbies were silent. Some park rangers began carrying guns. Their original role was protecting the public from wild animals, but this soon changed to protecting the animals from people. Now their task is to protect the people from one another. Smokey the Bear carries a six-gun. In many cities Halloween is being cancelled for the protection of children who have been receiving razor blades in apples, needles in candy bars, and hallucinogenic drugs in gumdrops.

The market in home protection devices is booming. There are call buttons to the police station, booby-trapped windows, home radar systems, and new housing developments boast 24-hour security guards. Police cars drive down the sidewalk in public parks and through the milling crowds at the state fair or any large public gathering. Always in pairs and unsmiling, they carry guns and riot gear. If you try to say hello, they reply sheepishly or not at all, as if you had caught them somewhere they shouldn't be. They are particularly watchful of young people whose gregarious behavior seems covered by five different misdemeanor charges and a possible felony of conspiring to congregate. A single loiterer is a potential mob because he is likely to be joined by others of similar disposition.

There are uniformed security guards at every shopping center (a rent-a-cop looks like a policeman but is attached to a private agency). In California they want themselves classified as peace officers, a move strongly resisted by the regular law enforcement officials who have enough trouble as it is. At a time when police complain about their public image, it is curious to see all these other groups including university security officers, attempting to classify themselves legally as police officers. Many of the residential streets in suburban areas have signs announcing that they are privately patroled 24 hours a day. These rent-a-cops operate like bounty hunters and receive $150 bonus for every crook they catch.

There are TV cameras everywhere. Smaller stores still use the big parabolic mirrors, but all the larger stores and corporations have switched to television. Somewhere in the bowels of every large building is a uniformed man scanning a bank of TV screens. One can only wonder how much TV he watches at home. Several cities have entire streets monitored by TV. Transparent telephone booths along the public thoroughfare and public parks are designed to provide visual access for cruising patrol cars. The wide interior sidewalks of new parks may be a convenience for bicycles and baby carriages, but they are really intended for police cars.

Although the average citizen can get by with three doorlocks and an elaborate alarm system, identification numbers on all his possessions, several loaded guns readily available in the house, and a private neighborhood patrol, more elaborate security measures are required for public officials. The president and his chief advisors, whose itineraries are planned with military precision, fly in special planes from military airports, ride through the countryside in armored limousines, and speak at public gatherings behind bulletproof glass with armed secret service men on either side. The chief executive is no longer free to walk among the citizens whose interests he represents. This trend seeps down to his immediate subordinates and their families. Bodyguards are not sufficient for Secretary of Labor Peter Brennan, who carries a loaded pistol around with him. Because Brennan often crosses state lines on the job, it was necessary for the administration to deputize him a federal marshall (without salary) to permit him to carry his pistol along with him.[5] State governors have been quick to follow the president's lead and establish their own guard to protect themselves from the electorate. Corporate officers and their union counterparts also have bodyguards. Career opportunities in the security fields must be excellent.

In a garrison state the enemy is external—the Russians, the Chinese, the revolutionaries, or the whole outside world—but in the security state the potential enemy is your neighbor. Psychologically, an external threat produces fear, an internal one anxiety. There can be a collective mobilization against other nations, a sense of shared national purpose set to martial music, but against an internal threat an individual arms himself and trusts no one, not even the government or the press, which have both been infiltrated. The barricades or ramparts in the security state are the boundaries of one's suburban lot or the triple-locked door of one's city apartment with its peephole conveying a convex image of the outside world. Many people are reluctant to open their doors to talk to anyone, including public opinion pollsters and census takers. California pollster Mervyn Field believes that the

---

[5] Robert A. Dobbin, "Brennan Gets Permit for Pistol," Sacramento *Bee,* April 25, 1973, p. A2.

fear of strangers, more than government regulations, will doom public opinion polling.[6]

I visited the data-processing center of a large bank. Security may be tighter at San Quentin, but I doubt it. In the lobby security officers walked by every 90 seconds; there was TV surveillance above, and the occasional appearance of plainclothes officers who eyed my briefcase suspiciously. To allay their fears I opened the briefcase ostensibly to look at some material, but really to show there was no bomb inside. Upstairs the employees passed through sally ports or "man traps" as they are known locally, before entering or leaving their work areas. These are double doors with a security guard in a protected control booth in the center. The entering employee inserts a plastic identification badge in the outside gate and this opens up the first locked door. Then he stands inside the sally port while the door is locked behind him, and shows his pass to the guard, who acknowledges it by unlocking the second door. This sequence is followed every day by hundreds of employees in these areas when they come to work, go to lunch or to the restroom, and when they leave in the evening. All the restrooms in the building are locked and each employee carries a special key. It used to be that only the top executives had special washroom keys, but it is hard to see in this new development a trend toward corporate democracy.

In his new security roles, man's best friend has become distinctly unfriendly. He stands at the border sniffing out marijuana, guards against skyjackers at the airport, and protects hundreds of thousands of city apartments where he is again being bred for traits of ferociousness and instant obedience. A few years ago it was sufficient to have a scarecrow to guard a cornfield. Now some farmers are using live guards with shotguns to deter not only the birds who aren't frightened by scarecrows but passersby who might steal a few ears of corn. As a boy in Pennsylvania, I could stop on almost any country road, scramble over the rock fence used as a boundary marker, and wander around the fields to look for berries and wild grapes. There was one farm in the area with a "No Trespassing" sign where they chased kids away— my brother and I always referred to this as the "mean lady's farm." Now there are "Posted" and "No Trespassing" signs every hundred yards and barbed wire to back them up. The situation is even worse

[6] Lee Frenstad, "Researcher Fears for Polls," Sacramento *Bee*, May 3, 1973, p. A4.

in California, where there are no informal places to pull off the highway and let children romp during a long drive. There is a barbed wire curtain along the roadway corridor so that the informal pullover or rest area has either disappeared or has been replaced by the antiseptic camper-dominated state rest areas.

In the beginning a person feels uncomfortable about the presence of armed police in the bus station or shopping center. Later he feels uncomfortable if he can't see a policeman. The same thing happens with the TV monitors in the corridors of the post office and some public restrooms. Initially they are regarded as an invasion of privacy, but eventually a person is uncomfortable when Big Brother *isn't* watching. Psychologist Kurt Lewin compared the behavior of children whose teachers used authoritarian and democratic methods. The important difference came when the teacher left the room. The democratic group got along reasonably well, but chaos prevailed in the authoritarian classroom.[7] One implication is that an authoritarian system requires constant surveillance of its citizens. If a policeman cannot be physically present, there must be TV monitors, citizens patrols, and remote sensing stations.

IDEOLOGICAL SUPPORTS FOR HARD BUILDINGS

Any effort to soften hard buildings and improve the lot of the public housing tenant, the prisoner, or the park user will encounter the popular prejudice against "frills" in public facilities. As they say about army buildings, "It doesn't have to be cheap, it just has to look cheap." The taxpayer doesn't want to believe that people living in public housing are better off than he is. Almost every prison official advocates individual cells for prisoners. The logic behind single cells is compelling; it includes the physical protection of weaker inmates, reduces homosexual relationships, enables better control of inmates in single cells, as well as increased privacy and personal dignity. However, whenever prison officials argue for single cells, they are accused of coddling convicts. The apocryphal question from the state legislature is how single rooms can be justified for people who have broken the law when

[7] Kurt Lewin, Ronald Lippitt, and R. K. White, "Patterns of Aggressive Behavior in Experimentally Created Social Climates," *Journal of Social Psychology*, X (1939), 271–99.

army recruits are compelled to live in open barracks. Is it reasonable to provide more amenities for lawbreakers than for draftees?

There are several good answers to this question. First we can turn to Florence Nightingale's dictum that the first requisite of a hospital is that it do the patients no harm. The minimum criterion of a prison should be that an inmate emerges no worse than when he entered. At present this is not the case and prisons are accurately described as breeding grounds for criminal behavior. When someone is hurt and angry, there is no reason to believe that putting him in a degrading and dehumanizing environment will improve his outlook or behavior. Indeed there is every reason to suppose that this will worsen whatever antisocial attitudes presently exist.

The logic of subjecting the poor, the criminal, and the deviant to degrading conditions is also based on a puritanical attitude toward comfort. A belief in the redemptive value of hard work and frugality pervades much of our thinking about people who are public charges. The first American prison was developed in Pennsylvania in response to demands for the humane treatment of criminals by the Quaker sect, a group characterized both by its humane impulses and a disdain for anything beyond the minimum in personal comfort. Following Quaker precepts, lawbreakers were confined in solitary cells with ample time to consider their transgressions and become penitent. The cells were quite large and the inmate remained in his cell most of the day apart from a one-hour exercise period. Later, when large-scale workshops proved more efficient than individual craft work performed in a single cell, the solitary system of the Pennsylvania prison was replaced by the silent system of the Auburn Prison, in which inmates also lived in single cells but came together to work and eat but had to remain silent. The idea that an ascetic life would help to rehabilitate prisoners was used against any effort to humanize the institutions.

Even today, efforts to improve the drab conditions of army life, to permit recruits to personalize their sleeping quarters or choose their own hair styles, are regarded by many senior officers as responsible for breakdowns in order and discipline. Not too long ago architects who planned college classrooms and dormitories were advised against making the furnishings too pleasant or comfortable lest the students become distracted or fall asleep. Guidebooks for undergraduate students still warn against too many amenities in the student's room. Here is a sampling of advice on dormitory furnishing: "Choose a straight backed chair rather than a very comfortable one. . . ." "All of the votes are in favor of a simple, rugged, straight backed chair with no cushion. You study best when you are not too comfortable or relaxed. . . ." "For obvious reasons, avoid studying on a couch, easy chair, or in bed. . . ." "A bed is no place to study. Neither is a sofa, nor a foam rubber lounge chair. When you are too relaxed and comfortable physically, your concentration also relaxes. A straight backed wooden chair is best for most students; it allows them to work at maximum concentration for longer periods." Before analyzing the attitudes behind these recommendations, let me state emphatically that there is no evidence that people work better when they are uncomfortable. Let the reader examine his or her own circumstances while reading this book. Are you sitting bolt upright in a straight backed chair or lying on a couch with your head against a cushion? My own observations of the way students read suggest that when a couch or easy chair is available, it will be chosen almost every time over the rugged, virtuous, and uncomfortable straight-backed chair.

Another ideological prop behind hard architecture is neo-behaviorism. Providing decent housing for public charges would be "rewarding" poverty or criminal behavior. The argument goes beyond the accusation of simply coddling convicts to the idea that improved conditions will actually "reinforce" criminal tendencies. Neo-behaviorism maintains that people won't be deterred from crime if the consequences are not sufficiently dire. This requires some form of punishment—if not actual torture then at least confinement without amenity. The critical question is whether confinement and removal from society constitute sufficient punishment or whether the transgressor must be punished still further during confinement. There is no evidence to indicate that such punishment exerts any positive influences on an inmate's character. Instead it increases his alienation from and his bitterness toward society. There is not much basis for believing that dehumanizing public housing will help to reduce welfare rolls, juvenile delinquency, or anything else society considers bad. Poor housing lowers the self-image of the tenant and helps to convince him how little society cares about his plight. This is not a terribly important consideration to a philosophy that is unabashedly beyond freedom and dignity. Hard, hard, hard, ain't it hard? Yes it is. But does it work? No, it

doesn't. City officials across the country will testify that there is no
such thing as a vandal-proof restroom or picnic bench. If restrooms
are built out of concrete they will be dynamited and have concrete
poured down the toilet holes. Vandals, thousands of helmeted Huns
riding out of the East, have managed to dig out concrete blocks and
haul away picnic tables weighing hundreds of pounds. Bolt cutters
and wire snippers can sever any chain-link fence manufactured today.
In the People's Park disturbance of 1972, the metal poles for the fence
were used to break up the macadam of the parking lot. Local police
were very cooperative in carting away the broken macadam pieces lest
they in turn be used to break the windows of local stores. The harder
the architecture, the greater its potential as a weapon if it is used
against the authorities. Prison inmates have learned how to make
deadly knives from steel bedsprings. Hard architecture also costs more
to adapt or remove. Pennsylvania's Eastern Penitentiary, built in 1829
was closed down in 1966, but has yet to be removed from the site because of the high razing expense. The extra costs of hard architecture
are manifold; first in the initial purchase price because it costs twice
as much as ordinary items, second in its potential for abuse once it is
destroyed as well as the greater cost in repairing or removing a heavy
and rigid item designed to be installed permanently, and finally the
human costs resulting from being in cold, ugly, and impersonal buildings.

Challenge people to destroy something and they will find a way to
do it. Many people prefer to ignore the great amount of technological
ingenuity released in wartime. Although only sketchy accounts of the
automated battlefield have been made public, it is evident that the
Vietnam War has produced the most sophisticated gadgetry in the history of warfare. If city agencies use remote sensors and infra-red photography to detect the presence of people in parks after closing time, it is
likely that such methods will have the same success in New York parks
that they had in Vietnam. Authorities who go the route of vandal-proof
facilities are deluding themselves. They are short-range thinkers who
cost everyone money in the long run. Adversity puts human ingenuity
to the test and the prison inmate naked in his strip cell is tested most
severely. By law the California authorities are required to provide even
strip-cell inmates with their own Bibles. The result is that the Bible has
become a weapon in a manner unintended by the most ardent mission-

ary. Inmates stuff the pages into the ventilator shaft and use the covers to stop up the Chinese toilet. Think of what the inmate could do if he had a table and chair to work with! An advisory committee on dental hygiene ran into problems when it suggested to the California Department of Corrections that inmates should be allowed to use dental floss. Prison officials pointed out that dental floss "when coated with an abrasive substance, could be as effective as metal blades in cutting through iron bars." [8]

The major defects of hard architecture are that it is costly, dehumanizing, and it isn't effective. Besides that, it doesn't look very nice. The prototype of hard architecture is the strip cell in the maximum security prison containing nothing but reinforced concrete poured over a steel cage without any amenities. If we can develop ways of humanizing the prison cell, perhaps we can also do so for schools, parks, and other public facilities.

The rationale of the hard prison is that the inmate will destroy anything that is provided for him. It is easy to prove the correctness of this view by giving a wooden chair to an inmate in a strip cell. It is likely that he will bang the chair against the wall until the legs have come loose and he has several clubs in his possession. Give him a mattress and sooner or later the authorities will have a fire or smoke problem on their hands. Just what does this prove? One can also supply numerous examples of maximum security cells that are equally secure and full of amenities including rugs, tables, desks, TV sets, and stereo systems. In prison disturbances, where inmates are rampaging against virtually every part of the prison building, television sets purchased with inmate welfare funds remain undisturbed. Nor do inmates destroy the paintings made by their fellow prisoners.

The arguments against providing amenities for inmates do not discuss the costs of denying a human existence to the lawbreakers. I have never heard anyone maintain that the inmate's mental or physical health is improved by a bare, unheated cell with no exercise yard or outside stimulation. This experience does not teach him a greater respect for the law or the society that maintains him under such dehumanizing conditions. However, guards legitimately object to providing chairs for inmates who are going to break them apart and fashion clubs

[8] Sacramento *Bee*, May 8, 1973, p. B2.

from the pieces. The typical solution has been to harden prison furnishings with indestructible materials and attach them to the walls. But human ingenuity can always find a way to destroy things that are physically or spiritually oppressive.

Another assumption behind hard architecture is that security through steel, concrete, and electronic surveillance is cheaper and more effective than security through public access. Stated another way, security can be gained through technological control of the environment. This is perhaps valid when one is working *with* people rather than against them. To design a highway to minimize ambiguity, error, and accidents increases everyone's sense of security. I feel more comfortable riding my bike on a well-planned bicycle path than on a street or highway that was designed with automobiles in mind. However, we have not been discussing situations in which everyone gains from good design, but rather those in which hard architecture is used by one group to exclude or oppress another.

The emulation of the prison as a security environment is the more ironic because the prison is a failing institution from everyone's standpoint. It provides no security for inmates, guards, wardens, and visitors. It does provide a short-run protection to outside society by segregating offenders for brief periods, but this must be weighed against the corrosive effects of incarceration in an oppressive and unnatural environment.

SOFT ARCHITECTURE

If experience has shown that hard architecture isn't working from the standpoint of economics, aesthetics, or human dignity, what then is the answer? The solution, I believe, is to reverse course and make buildings more rather than less responsive to their users. Instead of hardening things to resist human imprint, let us design buildings, parks, and cities to welcome and reflect the presence of human beings —let us abandon the fruitless and costly search for ever more secure cell furnishings. There is another alternative to the completely empty cell. This would involve materials such as foam and inflatables as well as other types of plastics. Provided one selects materials that are fireproof, the security implications of an inexpensive air mattress or styrofoam chair are virtually zero, or at least they are considerably less than with ordinary prison furnishings. There is no justification for inmates in maximum security cells sleeping on hard concrete floors when the wholesale cost of an air mattress is twenty cents. At least an inmate should be offered a choice between the bare concrete floor and an air mattress which he can destroy if he chooses. If he elects to destroy the air mattress, the security implications to the guard as well as the cost to the taxpayers are minimal. However, if he does not destroy it, an equally inexpensive foam chair might be tried next. In this way a valid transaction between the inmate and the authorities regarding cell furnishings could be established.

Soft architecture can change the relationship between keeper and inmate. New Jersey State Penitentiary in Leesburg was deliberately built by the architects to include breakable materials; a necessary adjunct to a humane environment. Glass abounds and each cell has natural light with an exterior window in addition to the glazed walls separating cells from courtyards. Locally some people refer to this medium security facility as "the glass house." All windows face the interior courtyards and exterior security is provided by the back wall of the residential units, a deep overhang of the roof to prevent climbing, and a cyclone fence surrounding the entire site. However the interior of the prison contains a great amount of breakable material requiring inmates and guards to reach a mutually satisfactory accommodation, because any burst of anger would result in shattered glass.[9] It would indeed be difficult to run a repressive prison in "the glass house." On the other hand, it requires tremendous tact, patience, and sensitivity to run such a prison. Let the reader answer whether he or she would prefer to work (or be confined) in Leesburg or in a traditional institution.

Several years ago, the dormitories on my campus had strict rules against students hanging pictures or posters on the walls. There were constant inspections by university officials who removed illegal posters and fined the offenders. The basis for these regulations was that the tacks or tape used to mount these posters would scratch the walls. The prohibition against decorating dormitory rooms continued for years even though it was a constant irritant as well as being costly and inef-

[9] Suzanne Stephens, "Pushing Prisons Aside," *The Architectural Forum* (March 1973), pp. 28–51.

fective. Besides the inspections there was the annual repainting bill, which mounted steadily over the years. Eventually the administration decided that it would be cheaper and happier for everyone to let students hang anything they wanted on their walls. The housing office now provides paint at the beginning of the year so that students can erase anything done by the previous occupants and have the colors they want. Students living on the same floor can decide jointly how the corridors and stairwells are to be painted. New dormitories now contain soft wall materials such as cork or burlap on wood so that students can hang pictures, mobiles, or macramé without marring the surface. They are built to be largely maintained by the users. This has proven cheaper and more satisfying than the previous arrangement of bare walls accompanied by constant inspections, fines, and reprimands, as well as periodic repainting by the maintenance staff. It costs $15 per room to allow students to do the painting themselves, compared to $75 charged by physical plant office. In 1970, the repaint rate was 10 percent—that is, only one out of ten rooms was repainted by the subsequent occupant.[10]

To the New York subway authorities agonizing over graffiti, soft architecture would mean starting with a realistic appraisal of the subway environment rather than viewing it as a symbolic representation of a divine social order. For as long as I can remember, these subways have been dirty, drab, and depressing. An official report to Mayor Lindsay described New York's subways as "the world's most squalid public environment." [11] No one can seriously maintain that graffitists ruined the attractive architecture of the stations or the clean lines of the subway cars. If the graffiti do not reflect my values, neither do the ads for Seagrams or the First National City Bank or the recruiting posters for the U.S. Marines. The answer to graffiti is not more police and watchmen or more stringent penalties against slogan writers. These are stopgap measures which serve to challenge the ingenuity of the graffiti writers. In Philadelphia Dr. Cool sprayed his name on several patrol cars. Sergeant Anthony McGuire of Philadelphia, who heads the special intelligence squad formed to catch graffiti artists, reports that his task isn't easy because the kids are using lookouts and are fast afoot. Several

---

[10] Robbie Hart, "Room Painting in the Residence Halls." Unpublished report, University of California, Davis Housing Office, 1970.

[11] Ervin Galantay, "Space-Time in Montreal," *The Nation*, May 1, 1967, p. 560.

officers have been injured chasing after wall scribblers. Edward Skloot, who is a special graffiti consultant to Mayor Lindsay, is more philosophical. "What can we do," he moaned, "we can't cut off their little hands, can we ha ha ha? It's getting worse every day. Hopefully it will all wear off—I mean the fad." [12] At last reports the graffiti artists have changed their style rather than their locus of operations. Subway cars are showing less of the "quick treatment" and more of what transit authorities call the grand design or masterpiece. A masterpiece is a large multicolored inscription done with cans of spray paint that may cover half or more of a car's length. I think that most impartial observers would admit that these designs are an improvement over the dirty grey or olive green subway cars. A cynical view had been that the drabness of the subway environment was done deliberately to enhance the appeal of advertising posters. If subway cars have colorful, attractive interiors, the advertising posters would be out of place or at least less compelling.

There are some signs of a more sympathetic attitude of the courts toward graffiti. A recent decision of the Court of Claims in Albany concluded that the state's failure to remove graffiti does not constitute negligence. Several black students had staged a protest against racial slurs painted on pillars. Subsequently one of the students assaulted another student inflicting severe eye damage. The victim's lawyer, in a $250,000 damage suit, argued that the state of New York was liable for the lack of supervision. However the judge said, "The phrases written on the pillars were disgusting and shameful, but they did not constitute a clear and present danger to the public safety as to require more than ordinary custodial care." [13] This is one of the first legal verdicts to decide explicitly that graffiti are not an immediate danger to the public order. Mayor Frank L. Rizzo of Philadelphia, a former police commissioner, however, typifies the tough line on graffiti: "This disregard of property rights may be a symptom of a wider sickness, I don't know. I do know that history tells us that when property rights are sacrificed, human rights are soon destroyed." [14]

The East Bay Municipal Park District, which includes Oakland,

[12] "The Magic Marker Strikes Again," San Francisco *Chronicle*, May 20, 1972, p. 17.

[13] Julius J. Heller, "State Not Guilty in Graffiti Attack," *Knickerbocker News Union Star*, June 9, 1972.

[14] "Graffiti Squad Wages War on Words," *Cincinnati Enquirer*, April 22, 1972.

Berkeley, and Richmond, has long been plagued with graffiti. One particular tunnel had to be sandblasted several times a year. In 1967 a Catholic priest was bothered by the racial slurs he saw in the tunnel and offered to paint a mural there. Park authorities quickly accepted his offer and supplied the paint. He did a colorful abstract mural that hasn't been mutilated or vandalized since it appeared over six years ago. The same priest set to work on a retaining wall near some tennis courts which was also a target of graffiti. He created a colorful abstract design based on some California poppies that were growing nearby. This wall has also been left alone by local graffiti artists.[15] Finally the park district turned its attention to the restrooms. Last year the district lost approximately thirty toilets, some smashed with axes, one dynamited, and the rest vandalized in an amazing variety of ways. The park district asked one of its own employees who was an amateur artist to paint murals on several outhouses. He chose nature scenes—pictures of mountains, trees, and grass. The painted outhouses have been free of vandalism since the day they were opened to the public. They are also, I should add, much more attractive than the brown outhouses in the rest of the park.

Jerry and Sally Romotsky, an artist and writer team in Los Angeles, have followed the activities of Chicano gangs who decorate neighborhood walls. Although the slogans and identity displays are continually replaced and painted over, genuine works of art by local people are left alone. Artist Arnold Belkin painted a large mural for a playground in the Hell's Kitchen area. Belkin was able to develop a large amount of community identification with the mural and there was not, at least in the report I saw of it, a single extraneous spot, line, or number defacing the painting. When a gang from 51st Street arrived one day armed with cans of green spray paint and threatened to attack the wall, local kids gathered in front of it and warned the invaders that they were risking their lives if they put one spot on the mural.[16] It is not likely that this kind of vigilance will be maintained indefinitely, but it is a hopeful indication of the sorts of attitudes that neighborhood people can have toward an environment that expresses their values.

[15] John V. Young, "Pop Art Gets the Upper Hand at California Park," *The New York Times,* June 4, 1967.

[16] Ernest S. Heller, "Ganging Up against Graffiti," *The New York Times,* September 10, 1972, p. D33.

When some anonymous individual painted cat faces on the storm drain outflow covers along the Los Angeles River, the city council ordered the cats painted over. However the cats came back each time the sewer covers were repainted. Eventually the city council surrendered and the cat faces remain a familiar aspect of the Los Angeles scene. They have appeared in many newspapers and on the cover of at least one book. The argument for leaving the cat faces goes beyond their cuteness. For one thing, the storm drain outflow covers are round with little pointed hinges at the top. They look exactly as if they were intended to be cat faces. Secondly, and of much greater importance, is that the Los Angeles River is the epitome of a hard river. The banks are solid cement and there is an endless gray cyclone fence on both sides of the river. The Golden State Freeway runs on one side and there is a tacky industrial district on the other. Although it is not necessary to argue that the cat faces improved the river bank (although a good case could be made for this) I dare anyone to say that they detract from it. The entire scene is ugly, ugly, ugly—the dirty little trickle of what once was a real river, the concrete embankment where plants and trees used to grow and wildlife used to run, the huge procession of power poles, and the wire mesh fence containing notices that the river is polluted. The work of the cat painters can be seen as a reasonable human response to an ugly and depressing situation. According to René DuBos:

> The greatest crime committed in American cities may not be murder, rape, or robbery, but rather the wholesale and constant exposure of children to noise, ugliness and garbage in the street, thereby conditioning them to accept public squalor as the normal state of affairs.[17]

Most of all, what the New Yorker resents about subway graffiti, and the Los Angeles City Council about the cat faces, is that these signs of human presence compel them to pay attention, to tune in to an ugly and depressing situation they had been conditioned to ignore.

On any college campus there is always a shortage of study space, particularly around exam time. There is also a great deal of unused space in the evenings, in the form of academic offices, laboratories, and even cafeterias, but it is difficult to get these opened for student use. I don't know of a single campus where faculty offices are available in the eve-

---

[17] "Life Is an Endless Give-and-Take with Earth and all her Creatures," *Smithsonian*, 1 (1970), 14.

nings as study space—the territorial feelings of the faculty toward their offices are too strong. However on a number of campuses there have been successful campaigns to open up the cafeterias in the evenings. These campaigns have been successful only sporadically and probably less than one-third of university cafeterias are routinely opened for evening studiers, another third are opened during examination periods, and the remainder are locked and available only during specified meal hours. The arguments against opening up cafeterias are custodial and security-oriented—the students will disturb the table arrangements and will steal the utensils and perhaps even the chairs and tables themselves. At a large university in Los Angeles where the silverware is automatically returned to the locked kitchen after meals, the explanation for closing the cafeteria in the evenings is that the students would steal the salt and pepper shakers. Like the belief that mental patients will flush magazines down the toilets, prisoners will destroy decent furnishings if they have them, or park users will chop up wooden benches, a few instances can always be cited, but the trade-offs in social utility and aesthetics are rarely considered. The best counterargument for opening up college cafeterias for evening studiers is that the system works on scores of campuses across the nation. The loss of twenty salt and pepper shakers and perhaps an extra $10 per evening in janitorial services to open up two cafeterias for around-the-clock use might provide the campus with an additional 15,000 feet of prime study space already equipped with tables and chairs. If need be, the student government or some dormitory organization can provide proctors or monitors in the late evening hours.

In all such illustrations—magazines for mental patients, amenities for prisoners, and study space for college students—the security and custodial opposition is largely specious, but this is obvious only to someone knowledgeable about the situation elsewhere. The argument that mental patients will immediately tear up magazines and flush them down the toilet has at least minimal logic *unless* one has worked on a psychiatric ward where magazines and newspapers are freely available. The arguments against amenity for prisoners seem equally ridiculous if one has seen maximum security cells equipped with carpets, stereos, green plants, and tropical fish. To the criticism that inmates will hide knives and drugs in flower pots and stereos, one can cite the fact that inmates presently secrete weapons and contraband even in the barest cells and sometimes as suppositories. It is also true that the majority of stabbings and other serious injuries have occurred at the most security-conscious institutions. The explanation always returns to the "type of inmate" and never to the type of place. The mental patients who had free access to newspapers and magazines and didn't flush them down the toilets were presumably a "better class of patients." Similarly, students at University *A* who have access to cafeterias for evening study and leave the salt and pepper shakers undisturbed are a "better class of student." This "class logic" treats people apart from their surroundings, as if there is some intrinsic self independent of the environment. This is a false model of any natural process, including person/environment transactions. There is no behavior apart from environment even *in utero*. People adapt themselves to their surroundings in diverse and complex ways. When those surroundings are cold and oppressive, people who can will avoid them. Unfortunately many people, for economic, social, or statutory reasons, cannot avoid places that oppress them. The result may be somatic disorders, anxiety, and irritation, but the probable outcome will be numbness to one's surroundings, with psychological withdrawal substituting for physical avoidance.

Personalization, the ability to put one's individual imprint on one's surroundings, is a prime ingredient of soft architecture. It too can contribute to security of property. When everything looks alike, it is very difficult to locate stolen property or return it to its proper owner. Following the lead of Chief Everett Halliday in 1963, police departments have been encouraging people to engrave names on appliances, stereo equipment, and other personal property. Putting one's personal imprint on a watch or toaster reduces its salability on the illegal market, aids police prosecution of those in possession of stolen property, and facilitates its return.[18] Experienced travelers have learned the value of personalizing luggage through decals or distinctive designs. Trailer owners are advised to "boldly paint a name or an identifying decoration on the outside of the trailer." [19] Such marking is considered a powerful deterrent because a thief is likely to pass over a conspicuous trailer in favor of an inconspicuous one. Another idea is to personalize the top of the trailer to make it easily locatable from the air. After

[18] Charles N. Bernard, "The Burglar in the Bushes," *Saturday Review* (May 1973), pp. 36–44.

[19] *Changing Times*, April 1973, pp. 31–32.

my last 10-speed bicycle disappeared, I painted bright orange stripes on its successor and bought a heavier chain. Anyone who cuts the chain and rides away is going to be very conspicuous at least until he arrives at the mob headquarters and repaints the bike. Personalization cannot prevent theft but it does act as a deterrent.

Cemeteries across the country are finding that they occupy a large percentage of the remaining green space in the city. Confronted with the pressure of people looking for escape from the noise and confusion, cemetery owners face a choice as to whether they should tighten up or open up. The view that cemeteries should harden—purchase stronger fencing, hire more security guards, and enforce trespassing regulations more strictly—assumes that the cemetery has the single purpose of serving the dead and their immediate families. This has not been a universal view of cemetery functions even in this country. In New England in the early nineteenth century there were many accounts of family picnics and town socials being held in and adjacent to the town cemetery. Celebrating and grave visiting were combined in a single day's activities. A recent study of Boston cemeteries showed a variety of activities being carried out by visitors, including pleasure walking, jogging, bicycling, ball games, golf and frisbee playing, fishing, berry-picking, and bird watching.[20] Counts were made of the number of birds living and nesting in cemeteries. In the Boston area alone counts showed 34 different bird species as well as raccoons, striped skunks, red foxes, red squirrels, flying squirrels, opossums, muskrats, and cottontails. There were also species of turtles, fish, and reptiles living and breeding in cemetery habitats. In the decision to open up or tighten up, the problem of vandalism weighs heavily on the minds of cemetery managers. The casual vandal destroys things seemingly without apparent reason while the professional will loot a cemetery of gravestones, statuary, and any item of equipment (including lawn mowers and watering pipes) that is salable.

Faced with the threat of vandalism, the cemetery manager can either obtain a sturdier fence and a more sophisticated alarm system and hire more guards, or he can attempt to open up the park to more public use and take advantage of the increased visibility to keep down vandalism. The latter has been the decision of the Boston Archdiocese,

[20] Jack W. Thomas and Ronald A. Dixon, "Cemetery Ecology," *Natural History* (March 1973), pp. 60–67.

which feels that decorative, inviting, and "see-through" fences provide better security to the cemetery and more protection against vandalism than the forbidding stone wall that allows vandals to work without fear of public discovery.

According to John F. Philbin, who operates the 37 Catholic cemeteries in Chicago, this policy of more public access and visibility has decreased the occurrence of park vandalism.[21] Neighborhood people now have a stake in the appearance of the cemetery and take a dim view of vandalism. Many cemeteries are enclaves left over from another era. As the ethnic composition of a neighborhood changes, a cemetery becomes a vestige of white culture in a black neighborhood or of Irish culture in a Puerto Rican district. The sight of Cadillacs and fancy cars from the suburbs returning to visit some of the last remaining green space does nothing to endear the cemetery to the neighborhood, especially if the cemetery is locked and unavailable for local use. It may not be too long before cemeteries follow the lead of state parks and charge admission. Forest Lawn Cemetery in Los Angeles already charges admission to some exhibits and has billboards along the highway showing a picture of Michelangelo's David—"See 500 art treasures in Forest Lawn."

The urban cemetery illustrates the trade-offs involved in hard architecture. On the debit side there is the cost of new fencing, security alarms, sentry dogs, and guards, as well as the expense to the taxpayers in the event of prosecution and incarceration. However, all this may be insignificant in relation to the denial of access to recreational space for local residents and the security state of mind fostered by the fence and the guards. The evidence relating security expenditures to protection against crime and vandalism is sketchy and ambiguous. Obviously if it costs five times more to make a cemetery 98 percent vandal-proof than it would to make occasional repairs and replacements, it would be better to open up the cemetery to public use and spend the smaller amount of money maintaining the place. However the equation is not complete without consideration of the benefits to the public of the open policy. It is difficult to attach a dollar sign to the pleasures of the jogger, picnicker, the safety of the cyclist, the nature study class interested in the bird and the animal life, or the history buffs interested in photographing old gravestones and making stone rubbings. Is the

[21] Ibid.

presumed decrease in vandalism with hard architecture equal to these pleasures that an open cemetery can bring to a community? The same question can be asked about schoolyards, parks, and public buildings. One way to prevent vandalism and crime is to erect fencing, install a sophisticated alarm system, and constantly patrol the grounds. The other approach is to make them more inviting, develop multiple uses to bring in outside people throughout the day, and give occupants a stake in the place. There can be no absolute answer to the question. There are degrees of hardness and permeability and trade-offs in every increment of hardness. I think there is a good argument against hard architecture on economic grounds alone—after a certain point it simply doesn't pay off in dollars and cents—but the strongest argument is the security mentality it engenders and the loss to the community in recreational space.

Some of the most persuasive data on this issue are found in Oscar Newman's *Defensible Space*. Studying public housing projects, Newman found a clear relationship between the form and layout of buildings and the amount of crime and vandalism. Because criminals work most efficiently where there are no people around, Newman advocates greater visibility over public areas including entrances, hallways, and corridors. He recommends that public housing should be created on a small comprehensible scale so that its areas can be controlled by the occupants. Security would be achieved through a greater sense of territoriality on the part of tenants.[22] Defensible space is defined by real and symbolic barriers that combine to bring an environment under the control of its occupants. This is basically the goal of the soft architecture approach. Hard buildings, however, are designed by professionals at the behest of one group of people (clients) to provide shelter for another group of people (occupants). In the process of design as well as in form, hard architecture denies occupants control over their surroundings. The space is alien, bureaucratic, and seemingly unowned by anyone except the custodians or some impersonal remote authority. It is devoid of personalization and responsiveness to human input.

Both defensible space and soft architecture emphasize security through greater visibility and occupant involvement. However, the main difference between Newman's recommendations toward greater territorialization and those dealing with softer and more responsive

[22] *Defensible Space* (New York: Macmillan, 1972), p. 3.

spaces lies in the nature of the buildings. Newman is specifically concerned with residential spaces where the notion of territory is appropriate. By contrast, this and subsequent chapters are concerned with public spaces where people are more likely to have *jurisdictions* than territories.[23] Methods used to increase the connection between people and buildings in public spaces such as schools, libraries, or office buildings will differ from those used in a residential environment.

In the public housing project there is not a great problem of graffiti *inside* apartments. Rather graffiti appear in the unowned public spaces such as building exteriors, corridors, hallways, and elevators. For these jurisdictional spaces we cannot apply Newman's recommendation of giving territorial control to the occupants. In a society emphasizing individualism and impersonal standards enforced by external authorities, community spirit is too weak to exert effective control. One must first develop a sense of community that would include some connectedness between people and their surroundings. For subway graffiti, why not ask some community groups in Harlem and Little Italy to create murals for subway cars? There is ample reason to believe that most of them will be left undisturbed by spray-can artists. Some murals are defaced but this seems the exception rather than the rule. Commissioning murals is a more creative and less costly solution than hiring more guards or purchasing subway cars from a manufacturer complete with graffiti comments on them. Elite irony will not solve "the graffiti problem" which I see as less the wall writing than the ugly and dehumanizing environment that provokes a human response. Besides making stations and subway cars more attractive, murals would provide an outlet for the creative energies of local people. There is ample precedent for pictures in subways and buses as long as they are advertising something. As the interests and aspirations of local groups change, new groups can be asked to create murals. If any of the old ones are worth preserving, this would be a fortuitous event that could be handled creatively. This is the sort of problem New Yorkers should be dealing with instead of forming police squads to catch people who create colorful designs on subway cars.

Subway graffiti are on the verge of becoming a pop art phenomenon. There is even an organization of street graffiti writers, and some Broad-

[23] P. D. Roos, "Jurisdiction: An Ecological Concept," *Human Relations*, XXI (1968), 75–84.

way shows have graffiti backdrops, exhibits, and demonstrations. Pop Artist Slaes Oldenburg finds the graffiti a realization of his dreams:

> I have always wanted to put a steel band with dancing girls on a flat car down in the subways and send it all over the city. It would slide into a station without your expecting it. It's almost like that now. You're standing there in the station, everything is grey and gloomy, and all of a sudden one of those graffiti trains glides in and brightens the place like a big bouquet from Latin America.[24]

The only real security can come from working with people rather than against them. Instead of installing more sophisticated electronic surveillance equipment in restrooms to prevent vandalism and muggings, we will follow the example of many European countries where there is usually a middle aged caretaker who makes sure the premises are clean and there is ample toilet paper in the stalls. For this the caretaker receives a small fee from every customer. In this country there is already precedent for paying money to use toilets in public buildings. Mowever the precedent is to pay money to a machine rather than to a person. I have never seen the crime statistics in restrooms with caretakers but my hunch is that it is extraordinarily low. The same applies to building lobbies where there is a doorman physically present. While it may be cheaper in the short run to install electronic buzzers and TV cameras, the long run costs in crime, insecurity, and the welfare payments to people who can't find jobs, as well as the expense of the gadgetry and private police services undoubtedly exceed the cost of the old doorman. There are many unemployed and underemployed people around, including handicapped individuals or those lacking the mental endowments to become computer operators and research scientists, who would be grateful for modest jobs in bus stations, restrooms, and apartment lobbies. In the presumed savings produced by electronic surveillance, no one takes into account the people displaced by the machines as well as the frustrations of people denied an opportunity to contribute to society. Creating security through people would help to reduce crime and unemployment as well as increase community. There will be a price to be paid in "privacy" but it is not clear to me that the presence of a middle aged

---

[24] Richard Goldstein, "This Thing Has Gotten Completely out of Hand," *New York,* March 26, 1973, pp. 35–39. See also "The Graffiti Hit Parade," *New York,* March 26, 1973, pp. 32–34.

man (or woman) in a restroom would be more of an intrusion than a TV camera. Our notions of privacy built into ever harder buildings borders on the verge of a national paranoia.

Soft architecture means increasing the permeability of buildings, opening them up rather than closing them off. It is based on the belief that the best sort of security comes from the occupants themselves albeit backed up by an adequate police force. Constant police patrols and curfews and alarms did not provide as good a level of security for New York's Central Park as the policy of opening up the park to more people more of the time. I am not opposed to police patrols because any large city will have its share of antisocial individuals, but these security aspects must be kept in perspective with the realization that the first purpose of a park is to provide green spaces for people. If parks are made ugly and unfriendly, their whole purpose disappears.

Fines against littering are both necessary and desirable but they are not sufficient. Without public support they are bound to fail. The New York City subways have had fines for littering for decades and they are still filthy. The Montreal Metro and the Moscow subway also fine people for littering but are clean, if not spotless. The difference is that Montreal and Moscow riders respect their subway environment and New Yorkers don't. New York's subway stations are dirty and depressing places. I cannot argue that the litter improves the environment but I will insist that people will not support antilittering policies in a garbage dump. Convert the subways into places that people can respect, and they will cease littering and vandalizing them.

In summary the characteristics of hard architecture are:

Lack of permeability. A minimum of contact between inside and out. The building has no connection with the surrounding neighborhood.

Expensive to construct, alter, or raze. Few possibilities for change or expansion without a gross misfit between building and activities.

Clear differentiation of status levels. Every activity and person has a specified location. Minimal contact across status levels or departments.

Passive adjustment and psychological withdrawal are encouraged. Little possibility for experimentation or change.

Rather than relying mainly on the occupants themselves to provide security with outside assistance when needed, security is assigned to a specialized agency. Eventual replacement of security through people by security through machines.

Materials and furnishings selected for ease of purchasing and maintenance, producing uniformity in design and layout.

When it comes to outdoor spaces, including parks and beaches, the parallel to hard architecture consists of hard regulations coupled with hard-line enforcement. There is the pervasive belief that the public is incapable of taking care of anything—they are presumed to be a bunch of slobs who will litter, cause fires, pollute streams, destroy natural vegetation, and slaughter wildlife. It is easy to document the amount of litter or pollution that unrestricted and unregulated public use can bring. However, the problem still becomes one of placing potential abuse in some perspective. The extreme solution would be to keep people out of the area entirely. However that is not the objective of the most vociferous proponents of the "people are slobs" theory, the owners of second homes at the beach or in isolated mountain areas. There is frequently a self-serving quality to these charges that the public will destroy parks and beaches if given the opportunity to use them. On the other hand there is the clear need for regulations and enforcement policies that will prevent abuse. The solution combines public education with reasonable regulations and courteous enforcement personnel. The public must not look upon rangers and wardens as enemy spies. The trend to hard-line enforcement policies exemplified by Smokey the Bear with a gun at his side must be reversed. Without public support, Smokey the Bear won't be able to do his job even if he travels in an armored personnel carrier and carries an M16.

The dream of a society in which people who share common goals will trust and respect one another is being suffocated in a torrent of concrete, steel, and sophisticated security equipment. I would feel less strongly if windowless buildings, barbed-wire fences, and electronic surveillance equipment were infrequent aberrations of paranoid homeowners and public officials, but they are not. Housing projects, schools, playgrounds, courtrooms, and commercial buildings reveal the hardening process at an advanced stage. If there is truth to Churchill's dictum that the buildings we shape will eventually shape us, then the inevitable result of hard buildings will be withdrawn, callous, and indifferent people. A security emphasis is being poured into concrete that will harden our children's children fifty years from now.

2

Symptoms of
Institutional Care

Winston Churchill also said that the health of a society can be diagnosed from the state of its prisons. Today in physical form as well as in rules governing the conduct of occupants, the prison has become the model for schools, housing projects, and commercial buildings designed for security and custody. Ignoring the facts of prison life was immoral even when only an underclass of prisoners was caged, but today as hard architecture spreads to other kinds of buildings, understanding the archetypal security building, the prison, is in everyone's interest.

Any attempt to improve prisons must be based on a clear understanding of what is wrong with them. Some of the problems in prison are similar to those of any total institution. The phrase "institutional look" has been used to describe both a type of architecture and the inmate's appearance. Sykes speaks of the resemblance between police stations, hospitals, orphan asylums, and other public buildings—"A Kafka-like atmosphere compounded of naked electric lights, echoing corridors, and walls encrusted with the paint of decades, and the stale air of rooms shut up too long." [1] Goffman's 1958 article on total institutions focused attention on people who became so adjusted to mental hospital, jail, the army, or concentration camp that they had difficulty living outside. [2] A critique of children's institutions concluded:

[1] Gresham Sykes, *The Society of Captives* (Princeton, N.J.: Princeton University Press, 1958).

[2] Erving Goffman, "Characteristics of Total Institutions," *Symposium on Preventive and Social Psychiatry* (Washington: GPO, 1958).

Institutional life has little relation to the outside world; it usually confines the children's contacts to members of their own sex, teaches them dependency on a hospital-like routine, gives them few work skills they can use outside the institution, and teaches them to live on a "welfare system" rather than to be as responsible as possible for their own needs.[3]

The process by which people succumb to the effects of isolation and routine has been called institutionalization, hospitalitis, depersonalization, prisonitis, and desocialization, but it involves several aspects which are summarized in Table 1.

TABLE 1

SYMPTOMS CLASSIFIED AS TO CHANGE IN PERSON OR OUTSIDE

Symptom	Change in Person	Change in Outside
De-Individuation	Dependence upon institution, loss of capacity to make decisions.	—
Disculturation	Acquisition of new values unsuited to previous community.	—
Damage	Loss of status, security, etc.	—
Estrangement	—	New technology, architecture, etc.
Isolation	Person and outside remain unchanged but contact between them is lost.	—
Stimulus Deprivation	Acclimation to new sensory patterns.	—

1. *De-Individuation.* This is the aspect of institutional care that has received most attention. It involves a reduced capacity for independent thought and action. The inmate becomes a so-called mass man, capable

[3] Elery L. Phillips, Elaine A. Phillips, Dean L. Fixcen, and Montrose M. Wolf, "Behavior Shaping Works for Delinquents," *Psychology Today* (June 1973), p. 75.

of little spontaneous activity. Coser has described the dependency which develops in a general hospital. This includes the unquestioning acceptance of routine and the tendency to allow others to make important decisions.[4] Using psychological tests, Ullman found that self-assertion decreased the longer a mental patient remained in hospital.[5] Abel found that mentally subnormal girls who lived in a constraining setting for the longest time were most accepting of authority.[6] Lowrie, who ran a welfare service for discharged prisoners, states that "nearly all of the ex-prisoners who applied for help were broken in spirit, unable to look their fellow creatures in the face." [7] Elkin describes prisoners who have become so accustomed to prison life that they become incapable of independent decisions even in small matters. The grossest manifestation of this collapse of self-determination is seen in those patients who dread leaving a prison or hospital and return quickly if they are discharged. There are many accounts of ex-convicts and patients who want to stay inside when their time comes for discharge.[8] Ellenberger describes this as a "nestling process." [9] Straus believes that Skid Row characters are cases of institutional dependency developed during early years spent in army camps, the Civilian Conservation Corps, and so forth.[10]

2. *Disculturation.* The individual acquires institutional values and attitudes unsuited to his previous culture. He may acquire a special vocabulary or language, as happens in prison and army camps, or an outlook on life that differs from his previous one. It is not necessarily a bad thing to acquire new values, but the farm boy who joins the army or lives for a time in a big city may find it difficult or even im-

[4] Rose L. Coser, "A Home away from Home," *Social Problems,* 4 (July 1956), 3–17.

[5] Leonard P. Ullman, "On the Relationship between Amount of Hospitalization and Self-Assertion," Paper presented at the 1958 meeting of the American Psychological Association.

[6] T. M. Abel, "Moral Judgment among Subnormals," *Journal of Abnormal and Social Psychology,* 36 (1941), 378–92.

[7] Donald Lowrie, *My Life Out of Prison* (New York: Mitchell Kennerly, 1915), p. 286.

[8] Winifred Elkin, *The English Penal System* (Harmondsworth: Penguin Books, 1957).

[9] Henri F. Ellenberger, "Zoological Garden and Mental Hospital," *Canadian Psychiatric Association Journal,* 5 (July 1960), 136–49.

[10] Robert Straus, "Nonaddictive Pathological Drinking Patterns of Homeless Men," *Quarterly Journal of Studies on Alcohol,* 12 (1951), 601–11.

possible to settle down again in his former community. Using Nettler's alienation scale, we found that although newly admitted mental patients have values similar to those of people outside, longer-stay patients have deviant values.[11] Later, when we asked a large number of patients and normal subjects "What is important to you?" we found similar results. Newly admitted patients gave much the same answers as the staff members; but the longer a patient had been in hospital the more his values differed from those of the normal group. With his increasing sojourn in hospital, "physical" needs (eating, sleeping, exercising) became more important to him. The reverse was true for social needs (families and friends, etc.), which declined in importance with long hospitalization, as did abstract goals in life (happiness, success, and good life). Dahl, who was a patient in a mental hospital, expressed this shift to institutional values aptly: "The problems of the world I left behind became less pressing than the small everyday problems of the world I now live in. The people I'd left—they too began to grow distant in my mind against the immediacy of those I live with now." [12]

3. *Psychological or Physical Damage.* There is psychological, social, and physical hurt suffered during a stay in an institution that persists after the person has left. Inmates of concentration camps often had their health so impaired that they require special diets, medicines, and care for the rest of their lives. This damage does not always seem proportional to the length of stay or the conditions inside. Murphy mentions a study of Danish resistance groups who were in German concentration camps. The period of internment was relatively short, averaging less than eighteen months, they received comparatively good food from the Red Cross, and had good conditions awaiting them on release. However, two years after repatriation, over 20 percent of them were suffering from severe symptoms. The damage can also be the stigma upon the ex-prisoner or ex-patient which prevents him from leading a normal life or finding a satisfying job outside. For adolescents, the damage can be the loss of schooling and work experience during the stay inside.[13] Spitz and Bowlby have shown that children who are raised in some types of institutions carry the effects with them for their

---

[11] Robert Sommer, "Alienation and Mental Illness," *American Sociological Review*, 23 (August 1958), 418–20.

[12] Robert Dahl, *Breakdown* (Indianapolis: Bobbs-Merrill, 1958), p. 90.

[13] H. B. M. Murphy, ed., *Flight and Resettlement* (Lucerne: UNESCO, 1955).

entire lives.[14] In England at the end of the World War II, the Curtis Committee investigated patterns of care offered to normal children living in institutions or homes other than their own. They strongly recommended that orphans should be raised in foster homes, or, if this could not be arranged, in "family group homes" and residential nurseries, rather than in large institutions.[15] The same conclusion was reached by Lyle, who studied mentally retarded children raised in institutions. He found that institutional children were particularly retarded in all aspects of language and speech, and in verbal intelligence as compared with similarly mentally handicapped children who lived at home. The same was true of personal independence—the ability of the children to dress themselves, to manage their own meals and toilet, and to help themselves and the adults who were responsible for them. He concluded that institutional care warps and stunts the development of already seriously handicapped children.[16]

4. *Estrangement.* The outside world can change drastically during the inmate's absence. A displaced person, for example, may find that his nation no longer exists. Inmates of any kind of institution sometimes find that their families have moved away or died. After years in prison, hospital, or even out of the country, the newly returned person may be unable to get suitable work. His skills may have rusted or simply become obsolete. One hospital where I worked had many patients listed on the files as "farmers." The hospital stood in the middle of the great Canadian wheat plains, but with mechanization and the development of farming technology, the term "farming" has changed its meaning, so that it now requires training and skills which their patient-farmers do not possess.

Curle describes the surprise and often dismay among returned British POWs at the extent to which their wives had become self-sufficient both financially and emotionally. Their places in their family constellations had either disappeared or been filled by other people.[17] The

[14] René Spitz, *The Psychogenic Diseases in Infancy* (New York: International Universities Press, 1951); and John Bowlby, *Maternal Care and Mental Health* (Switzerland: WHO, 1950).

[15] Curtis Committee, *Report of the Care of Children Committee* (London: HMSO, 1946).

[16] J. G. Lyle, cited in J. Tizard, "Residential Care of Mentally Handicapped Children," *British Medical Journal* (April 2, 1960), pp. 1041–46.

[17] Adam Curle, "Transitional Communities and Social Re-Connection," *Human Relations,* 1 (1947), 42–68.

wives of American POWs of the Vietnamese War have also had difficulty accepting the return of their husbands. Having managed their
families and finances for years while their husbands were in prison, it
was difficult to readjust to a man's presence around the house. The
returning POW, for his part, felt like a fifth wheel.[18]

A man who had spent three years in orthopedic hospital as a boy
describes his return home: "All my former insecurities assailed me, for
I return an alien; I held a passport indeed, but it had ceased to be
valid long since. Within three years a community to which I should
have belonged, had become self-sufficient, and so had I in relation to
it. A place had to be made for me, but I felt, and was, an intruder in
it." [19]

5. *Isolation.* The inmate can lose contact with the outside and be
forgotten by family, friends, and community. This accounts for the
phenomenon of the "well patient" and the long-term convict who is
denied parole because he has no place to go. In our research we have
found that the longer a patient remains in hospital, the more likely he
is to lose contact with home and family. After about a year, there is a
sharp drop in the number of letters and visitors and this decline becomes steeper the longer a patient has been in hospital.[20] Some prisons
aggravate the prisoner's isolation by limiting or even totally preventing
contact with the outside.

Isolation can be fostered and aggravated because the inmate feels
that those at home don't understand what he has endured. He may
stop writing "because there is nothing to write about that makes sense
to people outside." Curle describes how some British ex-POWs left
their families and became wanderers because they felt that no one
understood them or could grasp what they had been through. To cover
cases of this sort, Newman[21] distinguishes between symptoms that develop in POW camps such as those described by Vischer[22] in his book

[18] Stuart Auerbach, "POWs Were Sicker Than First Realized," Sacramento *Bee,*
June 2, 1973, p. A8.

[19] Anonymous, in *Disabilities and How to Live with Them* (London: The Lancet
Publishing Co., 1952), p. 229.

[20] Robert Sommer, "Letter-writing in a Mental Hospital," *American Journal of
Psychiatry,* 115 (1958), 514–17. See also Robert Sommer, "Visitors to Mental Hospitals," *Mental Hygiene,* 43 (January 1959), 8–15.

[21] P. H. Newman, "The Prisoner-of-War Mentality," *British Medical Journal*
(Jan. 1, 1944), pp. 8–10.

[22] A. L. Vischer, *Die Stacheldraht-Krankheit* (Zurich: Rascher, 1918).

Barbed-Wire Disease and those that appear immediately after release. He uses an analogy from medicine of caisson disease. The bodies of workmen who are inside caissons used in tunnelling under water adapt themselves satisfactorily to an abnormally high pressure much above that in the atmosphere. While working in caissons, men have no abnormal symptoms, but once they are released and the pressure falls, they develop the bends, an exquisitely painful and dangerous condition, due to the rapid release of nitrogen bubbles from the blood.

6. *Stimulus Deprivation*. During his stay in an institution, a person must accustom himself to a life whose tempo differs greatly from that outside. Headaches, sleep difficulties, and nervous tension are all common among people recently discharged from institutions. The first trip by car or train, which is often the transition from the ordered and sluggish pace of an institution to the quick-moving world outside, can be frightening. Two accounts by former prisoners are fairly typical in this respect:

> A number of men who have served long sentences in prison told me they felt the same way; they found it impossible to sleep during the first week following release because they revelled too much in hearing, seeing, tasting and feeling. . . . The noise on Market Street distressed me, and besides, my eyes pained. They were so unused to see rapidly moving vehicles and so many strange faces.[23]
>
> The world was strange and a little frightening; the traffic roared and pounced, the colors of women's dresses, flowers, and neon signs jabbed the nerves of my eyes, and music had a rich, new texture as tangible as fur or silk. I woke at dawn, and began to long for bed at dinner time. When I saw my first egg, I was stricken with awe at the impregnable perfection of its shape, so that I hardly dared to crack it with my spoon. When I saw my first daffodil I felt like weeping.[24]

It is not surprising that Lowrie compares the discharged prisoner to Rip Van Winkle or Robinson Crusoe. Reports from mental hospitals that have recently opened their doors mention that patients complain about the great speed at which cars move and that people walk too quickly. The inmate is often restricted to a visual world of few colors, institutional buff or prison gray. Katz studied the color preferences of mental patients, and found that short-stay patients preferred

---

[23] Lowrie, *My Life Out of Prison*, p. 39.
[24] Peter Wildeblood, *Against the Law* (New York: Julian Messner, 1959), p. 172.

colors with the shorter wave lengths (reds and yellows), while the longer
wave lengths (blues and greens) were more popular with long-stay patients. This suggests that the senses are deadened by prolonged stay in
institutions.[25] However, there is some evidence in the other direction
too, for some prisoners maintain that their sensory acuity was height-
ened during confinement. This was especially true for smell and hearing. There are a number of accounts of people who claim that they
were able to smell and hear beyond normal range of experience during
confinement. Some complaints about noise or about odors from the
food or toilets may be partially due to sensory *enhancement*.

The need for a stimulating and pleasing environment is most urgent
in maximum security and isolation areas. Inmates in a community
facility who can work in town or visit outside can obtain their quota
of stimulation this way. But in isolation or locked cells, inmates' minds
tend to wander. The lack of reading in prisons is often attributed to
the "kind of inmate" who is there—uneducated and unintellectual.
At least some of this inertia may be due to the drab institutional surroundings. Here is the statement of an educated prisoner who found
himself unable to do much reading:

> The thought of leaving prison a well-read man was smugly satisfying.
> Then I discovered that reading—reading intelligently—in prison is not
> easy, because one of the most difficult things to do in prison is to con-
> centrate.[26]

Poor lighting and arbitrary "lights out" policies are more immediate reasons why inmates read so little. A recent study of the Polk Youth
Center in North Carolina showed that the general light level during
evenings was thirty foot-candles and in the lower bunk beds was much
less than this.[27] The minimum acceptable light standard for reading
and writing in institutional buildings is seventy-five foot-candles.[28]
However the investigator found that in spite of the poor lighting and

[25] S. E. Katz, "Color Preferences in the Insane," *Journal of Abnormal and Social Psychology*, 26 (1931), 203–209.

[26] Anthony Heckstall-Smith, *Eighteen Months* (London: Allen Wingate, 1954), p. 32.

[27] Larry Goldblatt, "Architecture, Prisons, and People." Unpublished Manuscript, Department of Urban Studies, M.I.T., 1972.

[28] Faber Birren, "Dynamics of Seeing and Problems of Illumination," *Environmental Abstracts* (Ann Arbor, 1965), p. 91.

the distracting noise, some inmates do force themselves to read and if given better conditions and more reading matter, would read more.

THE PATHOLOGY OF CROWDING

Prisoners have a selfish interest in research into crowding, because they are so often the unwilling victims of it, but the long-range benefits of such research go far beyond the prison system. Thanks to the work of biologists such as John Calhoun[29] and J. J. Christian[30] we are learning a great deal about the effects of crowding on animal populations. Death rates increase, reproductive cycles are disrupted, sexual aberrations are common, and the customary social order breaks down. Although it is tempting to generalize from these studies to human populations, there are many risks in this procedure. On the other hand, we have very little systematic and useable information on the effects of crowding on human populations. Virtually every description of extreme overcrowding—slave ships, concentration camps, or mine disasters—involved outside stresses of such magnitude that it would be illogical to credit a significant portion of the resulting pathology to the crowding itself. Crowded slums also have high unemployment, bad schools, inadequate health services, and virtually every other indication of social disruption, which makes it impossible to say what proportion of these effects can be traced directly to crowding. Laboratory investigations of crowded rooms or civil defense shelters have not fared much better. Generally they involve such short time periods that the volunteers are able to put up with the crowding without ill effects. Yet the accounts of inmates about prison conditions clearly indicate that they are bothered by crowding. As one inmate described the women's house of detention in New York City, "The building was simply not built for all these living bodies. . . . In my corridor we were two in a very small cell. Whenever you were in your cell, you were either on the toilet or in bed." [31]

[29] John B. Calhoun, "Population Density and Social Pathology," *Scientific American,* CCVI (1962), 139–48; and his "What Sort of Box?" *Man-Environment Systems,* III (1972), 3–30.

[30] J. J. Christian, V. Flyger, and D. E. Davis, "Factors in Mass Mortality of a Herd of Sika Deer," *Chesapeake Science,* 1 (1960), 79–95.

[31] Grace Paley, "Killers, Whores, and Jaywalkers," *The Village Voice,* July 28, 1966, p. 2.

Prison guards also desire relief from overcrowded conditions. The California Correctional Officers Association warned that overcrowded conditions at a nearby facility constitute "a serious threat to the lives of guards or inmates . . . an explosive situation that, if left unchecked, may well lead to bloodshed and possibly even death." [32]

The topic of crowding inevitably brings us to a question that arises whenever a correctional facility is planned—the *optimal* size of a single cell. It seems clear that this will vary from culture to culture, even from one inmate to another, and is influenced by the amount of time that the inmate is able to spend outside his cell. An isolation cell where an inmate spends 23 hours a day should be larger and present a more varied and stimulating environment than a cell in which an inmate is confined 8 hours a day.

There is some evidence from laboratory experiments[33] that women are better able than men to tolerate short-term crowding. However I would not want to see this used as an argument for reducing room size in women's jails but rather for increasing room size in male institutions. Although there is some validity to arguments against national standards for *optimal* living space for all inmates, there is ample reason to develop *minimal* space criteria. There are too many documented instances of inmates being confined in woefully inadequate amounts of space. The only feasible remedy as well as the most economical is administrative rather than architectural. It is absolutely impossible to design an adequate single cell that cannot be used for two inmates. Instead, one must develop a clear standard specifying adequate living space and defining the conditions for temporary exceptions. According to Richard McGee, a former warden, army prisons define standard living space as 72 square feet per inmate; this may go down to 55 square feet if necessary. It cannot be less than this for periods of more than 14 days, and not below 40 square feet in any event. The prison director must report directly to the base commander if the square footage per inmate goes below 55 square feet.[34]

Many states already have standards which they use in programming

[32] *Davis Enterprise*, May 15, 1973, p. 6.

[33] Daniel Stokols, Marilyn Rall, Berna Pinner, and John Schopler, "Physical, Social, and Personal Determinants of the Perception of Crowding," *Environment and Behavior*, 5 (1973), 87–113.

[34] Richard McGee, personal communication, 1971.

new institutions. In California a new dormitory in a juvenile hall is expected to have 50 square feet per inmate exclusive of toilet and service areas. The standards for juvenile halls state that the majority of sleeping rooms should be single, with a minimum of 500 cubic feet per room. But these existing standards deal with averages and often have no meaning for the individual inmate. At this time, the actual capacity of California's penal institutions is somewhat less than its rated capacity, but the maximum security institutions are still overcrowded. Statements about rated capacity have no legal force; they are merely recommendations about optimal densities. What is needed are environmental standards, particularly in regard to *minimum* spatial requirements. This is a high priority task for a specialized team consisting of correctional officials, social scientists, lawyers, and ex-inmates. I would not pretend that minimum space standards will be optimal by any means. Yet their existence will provide some protection to an inmate who is crowded together with one or two other individuals in a cell designed for one man. Minimal space standards would form part of an *environmental bill of rights* for prisoners. It would be ironic if such standards were developed first in corrections and then spread outward to the rest of society. Yet if the hardening process of the rest of society is following the pattern of the prison, it does not seem unreasonable that efforts to ameliorate its effects in prison will benefit people outside. I would not predict here the form that such a code would take—whether it would be a statute enacted by the legislature, an administrative rule of a federal or state correctional agency, or a requirement for federal support in corrections. Minimum space standards would assist harried prison officials in pressuring the state for additional facilities or faster processing by the courts to relieve overcrowding. The standards would probably be of as much use to correctional staff in reducing conditions that produce disturbance, contribute to homosexuality and assaults, as they would to the inmates themselves in improving the quality of life within institutions.

On my own campus, I have been concerned with space standards used in designing classrooms. For the past four years we have systematically evaluated student and teacher satisfaction in one particular room. People start experiencing crowding and a deficiency in ventilation when class size exceeds 17 students. Yet when we checked with the campus administration, we found that the *optimal* class size for this room was 25 students and the maximum was 31. This figure was supplied by the fire chief on the basis of local fire safety codes. I would not deny the value of adequate fire safety regulations, but it seems clear that there are other factors to be considered in defining optimal environmental conditions. Studies of the social psychology of crowding can have a direct and practical input.

HARD TIME IN PRISON

It may seem unusual to consider time as an environmental issue but this is essentially the way the prisoner looks at it. His task is to service time, mark time, and keep time until he gets out. The cell, the endless barred corridors, the exercise yard, the walls, all these exist to serve time. The special quality of prison time requires us to treat it as an environmental issue directly related to super-hard architecture. Time becomes the anchor the inmate uses to gain some stability and predictability in the unnatural world of the institution. The prisoner constantly calculates how much longer he has to serve; sometimes he knows this to the day and the hour. Cells contain rows of X's and check marks showing time served and time to go. "How long are you in for?" is one of the first things a new prisoner is asked. In one of the few serious studies of time perspective, Farber found that the prisoner's morale was seriously worsened when he was uncertain when parole might be granted. His suffering was less related to his immediate situation than to his time perspective.[35] As one prisoner wrote, "While you are locked up, your main concern is to keep cool and pull your time. . . . The way to make this time is to *ride* with it. . . . But the time counts. Even the dullest hour is an hour, and after enough of them you're through."[36]

Being forcibly confined and isolated from society changes an inmate's outlook in many ways. His virtual obsession with time is not easy for an outsider to understand. Only when we gain such understanding can we begin to grasp the strong negative reaction that many

[35] M. L. Farber, "Suffering and Time Perspective of the Prisoner," *University of Iowa Studies in Child Welfare*, XX (1944), 155–227.

[36] Chandler Davis, "So You are Going to Prison," *The Nation*, December 3, 1960, p. 437.

inmates show toward the indeterminate sentence. When I first heard of the indeterminate sentence it sounded like a very humane and logical device. Yet from the inmate's standpoint, it takes away his single anchor, his one way of measuring reality. He doesn't know whether he will have to serve two more years or five. It is debatable whether the possibility of earlier release outweighs the anxiety and uncertainty generated by the indeterminate sentence.

There is an urgent need for research on the time world of prisoners. To an outsider it seems irrational that a man would choose a flat five-year sentence over a one- to five-year sentence, but many prisoners feel this way. The explanation seems to go beyond a fear that parole officials will be capricious and prejudiced. It is connected with the experience of confinement and the need for order and structure in one's world. Not only must there be an end to suffering but a person wants to have a clear idea of when that end will be. As an inmate in a California institution wrote:

> Under the indeterminate sentence law, there is no fixed plan, no task, no specific date or goal towards which a prisoner can aim. There is no incentive for the prisoner to make plans of any kind. There is no indication to the inmate of what he might do to mitigate his sentence and there is no apparent rhyme or reason for the disparity between what happens to him and the fate of other inmates.

This inmate believes that the indeterminate sentence keeps men from thinking about the future. They live in a present world of gambling, sports, reading, courses, and anything else to "kill time." When the parole board finally does set their time for release, they begin to make plans with frenzied haste. All the years and months behind them now seem meaningless and purposeless. Nor can the corrections officials make reasonable plans for job or school training without knowing how long an inmate is going to be with them.

The administrative officer of the California Adult Authority in a recent interview described his views in this way: "A man who was sentenced for five-years to life is serving a life sentence until or unless the adult authority decides it should be something else." Many inmates take a very different view of the same sentence, considering it a five-year sentence unless the inmate by his present behavior warrants further incarceration. These are obviously two sides of the same coin.

A brief visit to the prison particularly during a weekday may give an impression of activity and purposefulness that has no connection with the lives of the inmates and the guards. The same pattern repeats itself each day and the twin goals are survival and filling time. Heckstall-Smith, a journalist who went to an English prison for fraud, said:

> At first, the outward and visible signs—the clatter of the machines in the engineering shop, the rattle and thump of the sewing machines, the flowers growing in the carefully tended gardens in summer—give the illusion of purposefulness. But soon, as one day follows exactly the pattern of its predecessor, one realizes that nothing there has any significance. Everything is without purpose. This strange, grey, drab community exists only to kill time and for no other reason. Every one of those hundreds of men working away in the shops or on the grounds is concerned solely with counting the days until his sentence has run its course and the law has wrung the last drop from the rags of justice.[37]

A new inmate may naïvely suppose that someone is going to try to reform or rehabilitate him in prison but he soon learns that the important thing is to "do his time" and get out. The prison administration would prefer him to do his time with a minimum of fuss and bother. A good prison record will help a person at a parole hearing and means a clean ticket (no reported rule violations). This requires psychological withdrawal and numbness to one's surrounding. Everything the inmate does in prison, including sleeping and eating, brings him closer to release. Mental patients cannot view their activities this way. The prisoner can always say "Well, today is over, I am that much nearer release." The mental patient in the occupational therapy workshop cannot say, "Well, I've made a basket and it has consumed half an hour, I am that much nearer release."

PRIVACY

The lack of privacy, even in institutions containing only single cells, is an almost universal feature of prison life. There have been many efforts to counteract this by giving inmates keys to their own cells and lockers, designing smaller dining rooms, and reducing the size of cell

---

[37] Heckstall-Smith, *Eighteen Months.*

blocks. However the economies of dormitory living, particularly in minimum security institutions, are always tempting to the budget-conscious administrator. Other considerations such as reducing conspiracies and encouraging social relationships are often used to buttress the arguments for dormitory accommodations. The trade-offs in terms of reduced privacy are known but are not clearly documented.

Some institutions regard inmate privacy as an unnecessary luxury. Army recruits have to live in barracks dormitories—why not prison inmates? The answer is complex. The likelihood of assault, homosexuality, and inmate exploitation is much greater in the prison than in the army barracks. The recruit can go downtown during his free time and he has considerable freedom in walking around the base. I would not underestimate the needs of army recruits for some amount of privacy, but the needs of prison inmates are more urgent.

Architectural considerations greatly influence the amount of privacy inmates will have. The physical barriers that shield inmates from staff may foster the development of a strong inmate culture with criminal values. Norman Johnston recommends against "honor dormitories" and the squad rooms because they tend to increase the strength of the inmate culture.[38] Most wardens object to double cells because of the problems involving assault, homosexuality, exploitation of weaker inmates, and so forth. Several accounts written by San Quentin prisoners on the topic "My Home the Prison" express the concern inmates feel about the partner with whom they must share a closet-sized cell:

> To see a stranger standing on the tier outside your cell one day with a bundle or box containing his belongings, is similar to what must have been felt by the young Indian brides or husbands when, according to Margaret Mead, they met for the first time *after* they had been married!

These same crowded and barren cells represent a haven for many prisoners against the tension and potential violence of the San Quentin yard. On their free hours during weekends, many inmates return to their cells for a voluntary lock-up for a modicum of privacy and safety away from the tension of the yard.

Privacy in a single cell is not the same as privacy in a dormitory, and freedom from constant staff surveillance may leave the inmates open

[38] "Supportive Architecture for Treatment and Research," *The Prison Journal,* XLVI (1966), 15–22.

to exploitation by other inmates. There are degrees and modalities of privacy—visual, auditory, tactile, and olfactory. Sometimes privacy means absolute solitude, but other times it can mean getting together with one or two friends and chatting or playing cards. Among university students living off campus, privacy meant freedom of choice rather than isolation. Unlike dormitories, apartment living permits a student to choose the conditions under which interaction with others takes place. The other side of the coin is that this kind of privacy also leads to isolation and loneliness among some apartment dwellers.[39]

The technological means exist to create micro-environments which allow some degree of separation in group living. Students in college dormitories place their desks so as to minimize eye contact when they are studying. In a prison dormitory, the use of individual high-intensity lamps may permit each inmate to regulate his own visual environment without disturbing his neighbors. The placement of the TV set and the location of the bathroom will also affect privacy. In a youth facility, conflicts occurred:

> Because adjacent bedmates couldn't agree on an open or closed window, on smoking or non-smoking; the proximity of so many bodies led some inmates to claim discomfort from the smells of other inmates' bodies, real or imagined; light levels were so low on some bottom bunks that inmates would squint their eyes to be able to read; inmates who tried to go to sleep anytime before lights out had to contend with noise levels above 80 decibels and the jolting of their beds either accidental or deliberate.[40]

CONCLUSION

It is important to document the effects of crowding and stimulus deprivation in prison to the extent that this information can be used to eliminate conditions that confine, constrain, and oppress people both inside the prison and outside. Such research can serve as a cor-

---

[39] Fred R. Costello, "Living in the Community." Mimeographed report, June 1971, Housing Office, University of California, Davis, California 95616.

[40] Larry Goldblatt, "Architecture, Prisons, and People." Unpublished Manuscript, Dept. of Urban Studies, M.I.T., 1972, p. 52.

rective to studies of selective volunteers which have generally come up with negative results. Edward Thorndike conducted an elaborate series of tests for the New York State Commission on Ventilation and concluded:

> With the forms of work and length of period used, we find that when an individual is urged to do his best he does as much, and does it well, and improves as rapidly in a hot, humid, sterile and stagnant air condition as in an optimum condition. . . . We find further that when an individual is given work to do that is of no interest or value to him and is deprived even of the means of telling how well he does it, and is in other ways tempted to relax standards and do work of poor quality, he still shows no inferiority in the quality of the product. . . . Finally we find that when an individual is left to do his own choice as to whether he shall do mental work or read stories, rest, talk, or sleep, he does as much work per hour when the temperature is 75° as when it is 68°.[41]

The short-term crowding of human subjects has produced few deleterious effects.[42] Confinement studies using volunteers for periods as long as six weeks have also been uninformative. As part of the American space program, volunteers were confined in simulated capsules and more recently in undersea chambers. The TEKTITE 2 studies are instructive in this regard. TEKTITE 2 is a four-room dwelling created from two 12-ft-diameter cylinders joined by a tunnel, placed under water approximately 600 feet offshore. Electricity, drinking water, and communication were received through cables. There was round-the-clock monitoring of individual and group performance. Based on their observations, psychologists concluded that "both male and female Aquanauts can adapt successfully to life in a confined environment such as the TEKTITE 2. Not only can individuals cope effectively with confinement and isolation, they can also perform work roles effectively in such a setting. The amount of work accomplished by the Aquanauts was great—probably surpassing the average daily time expenditure

[41] Edward L. Thorndike, W. A. McCall, and J. C. Chapman, "Ventilation in Relation to Mental Work," *Teachers College Contributions to Education*, LXXVIII (1916), 82.

[42] J. Freedman, S. Klevansky, and P. Ehrlich, "The Effect of Crowding on Human Task Performance," *Journal of Applied Social Psychology*, 1 (1971), 7–25. See also Stokols et al., "Physical, Social, and Personal Determinants of the Perception of Crowding."

of most scientists and engineers in normal, terrestrial environments." [43]

The extent of human adaptiveness to noxious conditions may be an important issue for NASA, but I am not sure of its relevance for the county hospital or city jail. It seems facile to argue that because astronauts and aquanauts can tolerate confinement and crowding with seeming equanimity, prison inmates can do the same.

The issues in crowding and captivity are connected less with pathology (how much and what kinds) as with the quality of life. How do we want to live ourselves and how do we want other people to live? The fact that institutions that confine and oppress produce pathological behaviors seems more an argument for eliminating such places than for continuing them as laboratories.

[43] R. Helmreich, "The TEKTITE Human Behavior Program," in *Scientists in the Sea: TEKTITE 2*, ed. J. W. Miller and J. Vanderwalker (Washington, D.C.: Government Printing Office, 1971).

3

Models and Fads
in Prison Design

The call is out again for prison reform. This seems to occur every twenty years. In spite of this, nothing seems to really change. One reason is the lack of any consensus as to what imprisonment is supposed to accomplish. One of the most important developments in mental hospitals twenty-five years ago was the distinction between the therapeutic and custodial missions of the institution. However, correctional facilities should not emulate a therapeutic model that was appropriate for mental hospitals, even though this might temporarily result in a more humane atmosphere in prisons. Converting the large isolated prisons into mental hospitals, as some might advocate, would ignore the fact that the large isolated mental hospitals are themselves closing down. A more serious objection is that the medical model is not appropriate for the prison. One director of corrections wanted to build several maximum security facilities for "treating" violent offenders, moving inmates from the regular prisons to these new facilities for ninety-day "treatments," after which they would be returned to the main-line prisons presumably cured or with their violent impulses reduced. There is no known medical treatment for violent or predatory offenders apart from surgical intervention and compulsory drug therapy, both of which the courts are looking upon in an increasingly skeptical manner when applied on an involuntary basis. The courts are also questioning the validity of "informed consent" for drugs or psychosurgery in a prison system where parole hinges on the arbitrary decision of prison authorities. The largest single source of outside income available to inmates in one California correctional facility is participation in medical experiments which yielded them over $200,000 in 1972.

However this activity is medical research and not medical treatment. This makes it necessary to develop models for correctional institutions that are specific to corrections rather than borrowed from other settings such as medical or educational institutions.

When models are vague and ambiguous, a situation described by Humphry Osmond as a "model muddle," they will be applied badly and inconsistently.[1] Here are some of the different images evoked by the concept of prison. The list is not intended to be exhaustive and it omits some of the cliché concepts like torture chamber and pleasure palace which don't contribute very much to serious discussions about improving prison conditions.

1. Warehouse. The prison or jail is considered a storage facility where people are put "on ice" for varying periods of time. Little attention is given to a program or change process. In its most humane form, this approach assumes that separation from the outside world constitutes punishment for a crime and a deterrent against future wrongdoing. For the architect the problem becomes a technical matter of fitting a specified number of inmate stations into a given amount of space at a desired level of internal and peripheral security.

2. Monastery. Although very few people want to see inmates abused physically, there are still vestiges of this attitude when it comes to providing even a minimum of amenities for inmates. Some people will make the case for a drab and spartan prison environment to remind the inmate where he is, what he has done, and how low he has fallen. This philosophy has also been applied to alcoholics in hospital settings where the staff insisted that they live on the same ward as schizophrenics to demonstrate that they too were sick people. The alcoholics invariably missed the message and segregated themselves from the schizophrenics. I do not know of any evidence that a drab or ugly correctional environment is in anyone's interest—the inmate's, the staff's, or society's. Accounts of men who have spent time in strip cells show resentment rather than repentance, anger rather than reflection.

---

[1] With his colleague Miriam Siegler, Osmond is developing models for illness and deviant behavior. This task, when completed, will help make some sense out of our conceptions of illness-badness-disability and cure-punishment-reablement. The models described here, developed independently by the writer, deal with the physical form and the layout of facilities for handling offenders rather than the conceptualization of criminal behavior.

When a person is hurt and angry, these feelings should not be compounded by putting him in conditions of utter squalor.

3. Motel. The goal is to provide each inmate with all the amenities that would be found in a good motel room—a comfortable bed, easy chair, bureau, TV, a private bathroom, and even individual temperature controls. This model need not specify the level of security outside the inmate's room or what kinds of common spaces are provided.

4. Apartment. In addition to all the features of a good motel room, the inmate is also provided with food storage and cooking facilities. This could be cooking as it is practiced in the free world or it could be some modified institutional variety that provides the inmate with a number of prepared frozen meals at the beginning of the week, selected from a list provided by the central kitchen, and cooked according to own preferences. The inmate's cell could also contain ingredients for light meals and snacks of his own choosing.

There is no restriction on the size or the location of a motel- or apartment-type facility. It could be any size and located in a rural, urban, or suburban setting and involving any level of peripheral security.

5. Boarding house. Here one aims at a small number of people, probably no more than twenty, who occupy a single residence and share such common facilities as bathroom, lounges, and kitchen facilities if any. Inmate rooms are private or semiprivate and open into the common facilities. The level of security encompasses the total residence rather than the inmate's room. The boarding house model is most appropriate for special-purpose facilities where inmates have something in common, and group pressure can be used to maintain order. There would be serious problems enforcing social norms with a constantly changing inmate population and no common purpose except propinquity. There are severe restrictions about the size of an institution using the boarding house model. In a penal institution composed of separate boarding houses, one would find difficulties in span of control if the number of houses exceeded eight or ten. The boarding house model is most suitable for one or two specialized residences within a large general institution or as a separate facility in a suburban or urban setting.

6. Community building. Compared to present-day facilities, this would be a much smaller institution, perhaps no more than 100 in-

mates organically related to the surrounding community. It is the model presented in the book *The Non-Prison*.[2] No effort is made to duplicate the services and facilities of a larger correctional facility or of the surrounding community. Instead the surrounding community is used to supplement the minimum facilities and services provided in the smaller institution. Its external appearance would not be too different from a convalescent home or a community hospital.

7. Colony. One could also strive to create a new community within the confines of an institutional setting. This could involve single-family detached houses for inmates and their families as well as apartment complexes. Inmates and spouses could be employed on or off the grounds but would spend their evenings within the confines of the institution. As a penalty for breaking the law, the inmate's freedom to leave the institution is curtailed but within the colony he would have most of the amenities and freedoms of people outside. Several countries such as Mexico have such colonies where whole families remain during the prisoner's incarceration. I don't know the effects of colony living upon the inmate's family but this would have to be compared with the present situation where the family is denied a breadwinner and frequently loses contact with the inmate. Apart from a few institutions such as the leprosarium, American society has not been too encouraging of such enclaves. The most recent development along these lines is the retirement community, but this involves a self-selected group of people of independent means.

8. "Just like home." This model is a delusion. A prison can never be just like home, nor can a college dormitory, a school building, or a motel. One can aim at the comforts of home without trying to re-create the inmate's home within the walls of an institution. Inmates come from a variety of backgrounds, rural as well as urban, isolated shacks and crowded city apartments. There is no logic in a correctional facility trying to approximate the inmate's previous physical environment any more than in trying to duplicate his previous social environment, both of which may have been pathogenic. But this does not mean that a correctional facility cannot provide the inmate with a humane environment rather than cold, sterile, institutional quarters. Warm colors, soft furnishings, and the amenities of a home situation are desirable without attempting to duplicate the inmate's previous

[2] H. B. Bradley et al., *The Non-Prison* (Saint Paul: Bruce Publishing Co., 1970).

home environment. A motel room need not look like a private home; that it look like a good motel room is sufficient. The same can be said for a hospital room or a prison cell. When a false or inappropriate model is used, the building, which is the concrete realization of this model, is not going to do its job.

AVOIDING A NEW FAD

When it comes to institutional reform it is risky to promise more in the way of goods and services than can be delivered. There may be a considerable lag between the appropriation of money by Congress or a legislature and the actual completion of a correctional facility. Any delay is likely to antagonize inmates and staff who must live and work in antiquated, overcrowded, and poorly designed facilities and who keep hearing about new buildings and improvements on the way. Disturbances can be expected when people's expectations are raised without tangible signs of improvement in their lives. There is considerable virtue in a low-key approach to correctional reform in which media publicity is limited until the value of a new service or facility has been demonstrated. However political leaders usually want their domestic programs to have maximum public visibility and more media coverage is produced by building twenty of something than building just one. This is a wasteful approach in terms of both money and the lives of the people affected. Why repeat the errors of a massive public housing program which replaced habitable slums with inhumane sterile towers whose effects on their occupants were unknown? Small pilot programs and prototypes seem a better course of action. It has been several years since the book *The Non-Prison* described community-based facilities. It is now time to fund a few of those in different parts of the country to learn how they work. We don't need to construct 100 non-prisons or even twenty of them. It would be realistic to try three the first year, evaluate them, and incorporate what we learn into three more two years later. Nor is it necessary to apply literally the architectural plans presented in the non-prison book. It is the concept of the small community-related facility that is important and this will be expressed differently according to geography, climate, and the nature of the surrounding community.

We need pilot programs and prototypes rather than massive federal assaults. We don't need a new approach so much as we need to try out many new approaches and find out the conditions under which each of them works or doesn't work. Instead of assuming that one solution works everywhere, let us plan for diversity of needs. The Hawaii plan has been described in several articles;[3] by all means we should try it out and see how it works, but we must remember that it is only a plan. Until it is tested we should not think of it as the prototype for every state.

There is also the rhetoric about blowing up prisons and the attitude of "Plan, don't build"—which has been heard before on the subject of mental hospitals. The former president of the American Psychiatric Association, Harry Solomon, was once quoted as saying that mental hospitals should be blown up. In the recent effort to close the large, isolated, and ineffective mental hospitals, many of which hardly deserved the name "hospital," the goal was to replace the antiquated buildings with small community-based active treatment centers. Unfortunately the legislators seem to have heard only half of what was said. When it was proposed, "Close up the large ineffective buildings and replace them with small active treatment institutions and community programs," all they heard was, "Close up the large hospitals." The result was discharge of many patients into the community without adequate programs and facilities for them. The burden then fell on the counties to provide welfare for former "corridor-sitters" who became isolated and passive residents of proprietary boarding houses. Perhaps the reason was that closing institutions seemed to save money and developing programs cost money. If this analogy can be applied to corrections, it will mean the closing of large state institutions and more people in county and city jails for longer periods. We have to ask ourselves whether this is a desirable goal in view of the present state of city and county facilities.

A recent Canadian study of former mental patients in foster homes has revealed a pattern of regimentation, inactivity, and social isolation reminiscent of the old back wards. In almost three-fourths of the homes, the boarders ate separately from the family and showed no interaction during meals, either with the foster mother or with each

---

[3] Suzanne Stephens, "Pushing Prisons Aside," *The Architectural Forum* (March 1973), pp. 28–51.

other. Many of the house parents had created separate sitting rooms for the boarder which the foster parent or staff rarely entered. In most homes there was a lack of any activities, partly because of the absence of opportunities for work and partly because of the failure to encourage personal initiative.[4] An investigation by a staff member of the California State Assembly disclosed some of the weaknesses of county-operated mental health programs. In many cases, the contracts provided for the patient's room and board but little in the way of treatment. At Napa State Hospital, alcoholics were removed from an effective treatment program and placed in an inferior county-operated program. Lacking experience and expertise in mental health matters, many counties overcommitted themselves to expensive in-hospital psychiatric treatment even for patients who did not require it. Bed care in a local hospital was found to be the most common—and expensive —therapy. With their funds thus committed, little was left to pay for newer, cheaper, and more experimental methods such as visiting therapists at the board-and-care homes. Finally, the Assembly analyst maintained, "the method of phasing out of state hospitals has been abominable. There has been no long-range planning on these closures. They usually have been announced only a few months in advance. If county programs do not receive sufficient notice on these, we can only expect the present situation to get worse."[5] The same issue of the newspaper carried an article on the imminent closing of a state correctional facility only ten years old, much to the consternation of the local citizens and the employees. No announcement was made about the sorts of programs that would replace the facility.

There is a deceptive logic to the phrase "Plan, don't build." No one has mentioned who is to supply the plans. If it is the same people or planning process that gave us the prisons we have today, there is cause for concern. One effect of the New Environmental Protection Act (NEPA) has been the creation of a new class of consultants whose major activity is writing environmental impact statements. These are often canned documents written according to a standard formula and lacking a serious commitment to environmental quality. There must

[4] H. B. M. Murphy, Bernard Pennee, and D. Luchins, "Foster Homes: The New Back Wards?" *Canada's Mental Health* (September–October 1972).

[5] Art McGinn, "Ignored Mental Patients," Sacramento *Bee,* December 10, 1972, p. C1.

not be a dichotomy between programs and institutions. We can try
them both in many forms. Nor can we afford to neglect the thousands
of inmates and staff working in existing institutions. These people are
in dire need of improved facilities and the courts are beginning to
back up these demands.

Few would disagree with the statement by Krishna Nehru, the
younger sister of former Indian Premier Pandit Nehru who spent a
year in a British prison for her part in the nonviolent resistance movement:

> Prison life does not reform, it only teaches cunning, lying, hypocrisy, and
> many other evil traits, making people unfit to live within a decent world.[6]

No one can argue that prisons improve a man or woman any more
than a zoo cage reforms captive animals. This is not some liberal illu-
sion about incarceration. At a large conference on prison architecture
at which hundreds of prison officials, sheriffs, and other law enforcement people were present, not a single person so much as hinted that
prisons reformed people or made them better. The justification for the
prison was the protection of society in keeping predatory individuals
"on ice" for several years. It would seem that suspended animation
would accomplish this more economically and humanely than the present system of prisons and jails.

Cataloguing the deficiencies of the present prison system is not difficult. Ironically, one can read a criticism of the American penal system
written fifty years ago and find it as cogent as any written today. Does
this mean that there is no hope for basic change in our penal institutions? I don't think so. For one thing, at long last there are large
amounts of money going into the criminal justice system. Secondly, the
reduction of the mental hospital population has established an important precedent for corrections as well as making available professional
staff experienced in institutional change. At a recent conference I met
the commissioner of a state corrections system who had previously been
the commissioner of mental hygiene. He had moved into correction
where both the need and promise seemed greater. Also impressive is
the number of architects and planners who have followed the dollar
bill into corrections. Whatever their reasons for being there, it is encouraging to see so many intelligent and concerned people directly

[6] *Shadows on the Wall* (New York: John Day Company, 1948), p. 116.

involved with the criminal justice system. Probably the greatest impetus for change thus far has come from the inmates themselves in protesting prison conditions. Following the disturbances at the Tombs Jail in New York City, some prisoners were found who had been in jail over 24 months prior to trial. They were crowded two, three, and four to a cell during a time which they were still presumably innocent.

The large isolated prison is not going to disappear overnight. The pressure from the courts system is undoubtedly a significant factor in effecting changes, because the notion of "cruel and unusual punishment" has been extended to include degrading institutional conditions. If the precedent of mental hospitals is followed, one can expect the older and more dilapidated penal institutions to close one by one over a period of several decades. This makes it terribly important to humanize the conditions in these institutions that will be accommodating inmates and staff for many years. Reform and revolution are not mutually exclusive. I would like to conclude this section with some modest suggestions for improving correctional environments. No one of them will by itself transform a prison from an oppressive to a humane place, yet any one of them will alter the institutional structure in a humane direction. Pilot projects and experimental programs are meaningful only when there is some commitment on the part of institutions to apply the results when they show promise.

This list of suggestions is not intended to be exhaustive or encompassing. It was developed in the course of discussion with a number of prison officials, architects, and others concerned with the penal system. If it does no more than jog the thinking of correctional people and architects to develop and apply new ideas of their own, it will have served its purpose.

URBAN RESOURCE CENTERS

The conservation camp has already proven a valuable tool in the correctional field. At Camp Sierra in California, selected inmates are given several months of forestry training and then sent out to minimum security camps under the joint supervision of the Departments of Forestry and Corrections. The careful selection of inmates is as important for the success of the program as is training in forestry skills.

The camps provide a valuable service to the state in maintaining forested areas and recreational grounds, particularly during critical fire periods.

One can imagine urban counterparts of the conservation camp. Rather than constructing campgrounds and forest trails, efforts would be directed to rehabilitating slum buildings, garbage-strewn lots, and neglected school yards. Inmates from urban areas might find this far more satisfying than cleaning up campgrounds in remote areas. As the program developed, urban resource centers might change from renewing the ghetto physically to working with human problems. There are many young children in the streets who could benefit from a relationship with an adult male. It is all too tragic that a disproportionate number of minority group males are in prison while children in their districts grow up fatherless and increasingly resistant to adult authority.

There is also an urgent need for the rehabilitation and restoration of urban buildings of architectural, historical, and cultural significance. It is noteworthy that the U.S. Department of the Interior is not only responsible for the National Parks Service but for historical and cultural landmarks as well. There are many buildings listed in the National Registry of Historical Landmarks that are in great need of rehabilitation. The urban landmarks concept could be broadened to include buildings that have particular cultural significance for the community, such as an old hotel where many single and retired men live. Such decrepit and condemned structures are uneconomic for a private individual to rehabilitate. The urban resource center could work with HUD and urban renewal agencies in selecting sites for preservation and restoration.

It is possible that these urban resource centers could become the vanguard of small community-based prisons. Just as park rangers and ranchers have accepted prisoners who will help control fires, it is likely that neighborhoods will be more receptive to prisons whose inmates help to rehabilitate old houses, play yards, and parks.

SERVICE VOCATIONS

Finding work that is socially and vocationally meaningful, personally satisfying to the inmates, and economically justified, has been a

Pruit-Igeo housing project in St. Louis: the buildings are being torn down because of the uncontrollable crime and vandalism.

University of California at Irvine: ponderous impersonal buildings set upon a bare landscape look impressive from the outside but are cold and inhospitable inside.

New York transit authorities are more concerned about the graffiti in the New York subways than about the general dreariness which has persisted for decades.

Painted cat faces are of more concern to the Los Angeles City Council than the ugly hardened river bank. Presumably, the problem is that the cat faces compel people to pay attention to the dreary river scene.

Large isolated mental hospitals like this one become warehouses
for people.

Patients become lost in the labyrinthine corridors and crowded
impersonal dayrooms and withdraw into themselves.

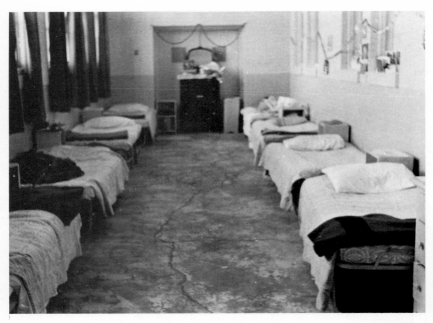

The zoo is a better environment
for people than for animals.

The design of most airports increases isolation and alienation.

With chairs bolted together and facing in the same direction, conversation is awkward.

persistent problem in American prisons. Most of the emphasis to date has been upon maintenance tasks—in the kitchen, laundry, or farm— or upon production of items for state institutions. Although maintenance tasks and production for state agencies have been useful in the area of job training potential, it is also true that the employment opportunities in production are not increasing as fast as the number of jobs in the service areas. Industrial technology has been automated to the point where fewer workers are needed, while medical technology has increased life span and kept alive more infirm and disabled individuals who need personal attention. Most hospitals, particularly those for the elderly or the disabled, as well as institutions for the retarded and mentally ill, are critically understaffed.

A solution would be to locate a small correctional facility near a school for retarded children or a convalescent hospital. The entrances of both institutions could be arranged so that security arrangements would be possible. Pilot programs could be developed that trained inmates in the care and rehabilitation of the retarded, the blind, the elderly, and the physically disabled. Such work may be more satisfying as well as vocationally relevant than existing prison jobs. From a practical standpoint, state-subsidized programs for employment after release are more feasible in service occupations (because the institutions are under state auspices or are largely state-subsidized) than in the production area in the private sector.

VISITOR AND MAIL POLICIES

Penal institutions vary greatly among themselves in the number, length, and circumstances of visits permitted. It seems clear that what is an overriding security consideration in one institution is considered a minor problem in another. A properly designed visiting area with inspections for contraband taking place in an intermediate zone between the secure prison area and the visiting area can reduce many of the difficulties. With proper inspection taking place elsewhere, the visiting area does not have to be hard and unfriendly.

Letters to prisoners also maintain contact with family and friends outside, but these are often slowed down or limited in number for security reasons. Again, institutions differ greatly among themselves in their mail restrictions and policies. It might be possible to design a letter form comparable to the overseas air letter, perhaps with open sides and light paper, that would be virtually contraband-proof. Such letters might go directly to the prisoner without any sort of staff surveillance. Such a policy might be very good for prisoner morale and also for families, who would not feel that their letters were read by strangers.

There should be a comprehensive examination of visiting and mail policies among various institutions. This would be a good project for an applied social research unit in the federal correctional system. As in the hospital field, it seems probable that visiting hours can be liberalized without creating problems of great magnitude. Many restrictions on visiting rest on the fear that the institution would be swamped with visitors on weekdays or evenings as is often the case on weekends. Several pilot programs on open visiting hours might help dispel these fears or perhaps reveal that they are indeed justified.

Another possibility, suggested by Mr. Richard McGee, is to explore the use of tapes and leased telephone wires for contact with the outside. Through leased wires a relative could phone the prison at any hour and the message would be recorded on tape and then passed on to the inmate sometime during the next day. Many inmates have difficulty writing letters and a tape system would be an excellent way for them to maintain contact with their families outside. It is possible that the Bell Telephone Company or one of its subsidiaries would help develop a pilot program exploring the use of a leased wiretape storage system for contact between prisoners and their families.

CONJUGAL VISITS

The architecture of many prisons makes a program of family visits difficult if not impossible. Apart from programs where the spouse can stay overnight or over a weekend, there are problems bringing in children and having play areas available when they come to visit. A number of prisons in the United States, Mexico, and other countries have conducted successful programs of conjugal visits for many decades. These cannot substitute for home visits, but for many prisoners without outside privileges they are the next best thing. On the basis of their years of experience with conjugal visits, prison officials in Mississippi believe that such visits keep down tensions that might erupt in violence, reduce homosexuality, maintain family contact, and give prisoners an additional incentive to maintain good behavior. Prisoners and their spouses are aware that smuggling in contraband or disruption within the prison could not only affect their own visiting privileges but the entire program as well.

There is a difference between conjugal *living* and conjugal visiting that should be expressed clearly in architecture. Conjugal living emphasizes a residential pattern, a house or apartment for the inmate and his family where they would stay for several weeks before he is formally released. In most cases these could be located in the city and make use of existing houses or apartments. Conjugal visiting, on the other hand, implies temporary one-day or weekend visits by wife and family, often to inmates who have no outside privileges. Here motel-type units within the same security perimeter that enfolds the visiting areas would be desirable. At present, many visiting areas are inside security control of the main gate, but outside the security of the inmate areas. This is the proper location for a conjugal visiting area, which should have play facilities as well as sleeping and dining accommodations for inmates and their spouses.

LIVING-LEARNING UNITS

Educational programs in correctional institutions have always been handicapped by a shortage of trained staff and classroom space. There would be tremendous value in self-instruction techniques, not only to compensate for shortages of staff and space but also to fill some of the idle hours. Programmed instruction is currently being used in correctional institutions, and one (Lompoc) has developed a teaching machine used extensively in the federal system and elsewhere. However it does not seem that any parts of the prison were architecturally designed to include the new educational technology. The result is that inmates often have to wait until they can be escorted to the educational area of the prison before they can work on their materials, and in these areas there is an exclusive emphasis on classroom instruction in basic skills. The extensive use of programmed instruction in correctional facilities would require some changes in state education codes as well as in building facilities. For example, to award educational credit the California Education Code requires 108 hours of *classroom* instruction. It is apparent that these codes were developed prior to standardized self-learning devices. Programmed instruction does not require separate classrooms, although it is usually beneficial to supplement self-learning with consultation with teaching staff.

TELEVISION

The use of television in prisons has been limited by the layout of cells and corridors. Virtually all dayrooms were planned prior to TV, and efforts to let prisoners congregate outside their cells in a dark corridor bring many security problems. The value of a closed-circuit TV system for educational programs has not been exploited for the same reasons. Television can also play an important role in any behavior reinforcement system. Perhaps the cheapest and easiest reinforcement schedule for an inmate would be the time he is permitted to watch TV in his cell.

Several manufacturers of television equipment should be contacted about instituting pilot programs in correctional facilities. The method used on some airplanes of having small individual sets in each unit is one possibility, another that is also used on airlines is to have sets at fixed locations in the corridor to be seen from a number of units with earphones in the individual cells. If the cost can be brought down, prisons would be a ready market for large numbers of TV sets that would also be used for educational programs. With a closed-circuit system, reading, foreign languages, geography, and the verbal component of courses in electronics, machine repair, or computer programming could be taught where TV is tied in with complementary classroom and laboratory experience. The possibilities of using television for an extensive in-house educational program are enormous. It seems quite reasonable that the television manufacturers and the broadcast industry would see the market possibilities of a small, inexpensive, single-channel, no-frills TV receiver for institutional use.

FLEXIBLE SECURITY

Whatever figures and projections in terms of number and type of inmates are used in designing a new institution, it is likely that they will be changed at one time or another. The demands upon a correctional facility change over the years as society's needs change or as new sorts of institutions are built that take over some of its functions. A good example is the treatment of the criminal offender with psychiatric problems where both working philosophy and legal regulations are in constant flux. Even if it becomes possible to transfer inmates to specialized institutions, there will still be a need for some differentiation system with a single institution. Unless the correctional administrator can apply rigid selection criteria, and few are in this position, he will not know in advance how many people are going to need what sorts of programs or security arrangements. Buildings must have some capacity to respond to shifts in inmate population and correctional programs. To design a fully flexible institution, where secure living units would be combined or separated, is very expensive.

A promising compromise between the need for flexibility and economy is the idea of *flexible security*. Although individual living units cannot be changed or combined easily, the security arrangements can. Hardware would be located in the buildings so extra doors or bars can be located at various points along a corridor or row of cells. When minimum security is needed, the doors or bars can be removed and inmates can circulate within and between areas. When maximum security is called for, additional rows of bars and doors can be added easily. This is a different concept of flexibility than most architects use. It is not the building itself—the walls or the structure—that is designed for changing conditions, but rather the security hardware of the interior. The building must be specifically designed to facilitate the easy installation and removal of security hardware. This is the sort of problem well suited to a systems approach such as that used in the School Construction System Development (SCSD) school design package.[6] The SCSD system did not provide the super-flexibility of doors and partitions that the teacher could move around at will. Instead it

---

[6] Educational Facilities Laboratories, *SCSD: An Interim Report* (New York: Educational Facilities Laboratories, 1965).

employed demountable partitions that could be removed or rearranged overnight or over a weekend by the janitorial or maintenance employees. A flexible security system for a prison would also involve one or two days' time for a conversion to a new level of security.

INVOLVING SELF-HELP GROUPS
IN PRISON PROGRAMS

One of the most heartening developments in the rehabilitation field is the organization of people who had once suffered from the abuse of alcohol or drugs for the purpose, not only of helping themselves, but of assisting others. In the drug abuse field there are several successful institutions for treating addicts run by ex-addicts.

As part of prison decentralization, several buildings or wings could be set aside for specialized programs by AA, Synanon, Daytop Village, or the Seventh Step Foundation. Security arrangements would remain the responsibility of the prison administration, but the sponsoring organization would have considerable latitude in the physical arrangement and layout of the experimental unit. The plan would require considerable advance discussion and agreement between state officials and the sponsoring organization. Contrary to what is often believed, many of these organizations are quite decentralized themselves and there is considerable variation among local chapters in the activities and interests of the membership. Although some local units of AA might be reluctant to supervise the day-to-day operations of a prison rehabilitation program, others would be pleased to do so.

It would be worthwhile to have at least one or two pilot programs involving a substantial number of ex-inmates as rehabilitation counselors. They should not be recruited as individuals but as members of self-help organizations. In order to resist the temptation of bringing in contraband or relaying messages, both of which they are likely to be asked to do, they will need commitment to group goals and purposes which can best be supplied through organizations such as Synanon or Seventh Step.

It would be logical for the self-help groups to develop marketing facilities for craft work produced inside the prison—such as jewelry, leather goods, or art work. Many prisoners do much more art work than they are able to sell at the prison itself. A Seventh Step house in a downtown area would be a good location for a craft shop. Synanon has developed several retail and wholesale operations which are economically successful and they would be in a good position to advise on marketing prison craft work.

CONCLUSION

This list of changes, most of them minor, is not intended to be exhaustive. An administrator of a progressive county jail described programs developed to use outside volunteers, particularly students, to work directly with inmates, run a child-care center for visitors' children, a portable telephone that could be wheeled up and down the tiers and plugged in any cell. There is really no limit to the number of creative innovations that could improve prison conditions. The present depressing conditions come about because one group (the inmates) cannot do anything to improve their conditions and another group (keepers and/or outside society) is unwilling or unable to do much. Prisons represent the epitome of hard and unresponsive buildings; but even here some of the above suggestions as well as those implemented on a haphazard basis in jails and prisons across the country can create a more humane and natural life for inmates. The essential ingredient is a determined commitment to improvement, or what Robert Hutchins has called "a questioning community" among inmates, guards, and governing boards. There is a limit as to how far one can go in humanizing a penultimate hard building before one decides to scrap it entirely, but I have never seen the jail or prison that has come even close to this limit.

The major issue facing the people concerned with the criminal justice system is not so much the form, shape, or size of prisons but whether or not there should be prisons at all.[8] There has been a general disenchantment with institutionalization of offenders. This is hardly surprising because it follows several decades of disenchantment with other types of institutions including the orphanage, the mental hospital, and the "old folks' home." There is also a widespread

[8] Suzanne Stephens, "Pushing Prisons Aside," and William Nagel, *The New Red Barn.* Walker & Co. In press.

belief that the general medical hospital is pricing itself out of existence. Although the idea of abolishing prisons is an attractive one, this is not going to happen overnight and hundreds of thousands of men and women are going to be incarcerated in existing facilities for decades no matter how many master plans are formulated. This means we must develop and implement reforms of existing prisons as well as formulate and test alternatives to incarceration. The fashion consciousness of many design professionals has been mentioned several times. There is a hypnotic pull to phrases like "community corrections" or "non-prison." I have been to "non-meetings" that were actually very dull "meetings" and visited prisons renamed "reception centers," "medical facilities," and "state colonies" that were all prisons. Tangible improvements within institutional environments are the goal, not simply renaming traditional buildings and procedures.

The vision of the late David Vail, a dedicated psychiatrist who transformed Minnesota's mental hospital system, can be applied to prisons as well:

> The mental institution holds a mirror to life. If we can learn how evil is done in that microcosm, we may learn how evil is done in the world around. And if we learn how, we may then learn why. More importantly if we learn how evil is done to the human spirit, we may learn someday how it can be undone.[9]

Although prisons remain the hardest buildings in America today, there are signs that other building types are using the prison as a model in developing security systems. The use of prison fixtures in parks and other public buildings, closed-circuit TV in garages, subway stations, and public housing projects, the use of "man traps" in banks and office buildings, high fences, electronic surveillance, and no-man's land type of guarded enclaves of suburbia have already been mentioned. This emulation of prison facilities might be more comprehensible if the prison were not a failing institution. Perhaps if we can learn to humanize the prison we can also learn how to develop a society without guards, often armed, in every bus station, department store, and public building. It is noteworthy that prison remains one of the few settings in which guns are never visible. This may come as a surprise to anyone who has never visited a prison, but it is true.

[9] *Dehumanization and the Institutional Career* (Springfield, Illinois: Charles C. Thomas, Publisher, 1966).

There are many uniformed men in evidence but they are not likely to carry even billy clubs. The ratio of guards to inmates is so unbalanced and the inmate society so well organized that any weapons introduced into the prison by the administration would quickly pass into the convicts' hands. The prison depends for its security upon remote force. In the crunch this means intervention by the state police and national guard. There are indeed armed men in the gun towers (San Quentin has recently added an armed woman) but their missions are surveillance and prevention of escapes. The internal maintenance of order depends upon unarmed officers and the inmate social system, which has a stake in keeping things cool.

The winds of change can blow from unexpected directions. Hediger's pioneer work in the psychology of zoo animals influenced mental hospital administrators. The laws against child abuse first became an issue in 1874 when neighbors complained that little Mary Ellen, the ward of one Mary Connoly in New York, was being beaten, starved, and mutilated. The police were sympathetic to the complaints but there were no laws under which Mary Connoly could be prosecuted. It was not until an officer of the American Society for the Prevention of Cruelty to Animals obtained a writ of habeas corpus under laws designed to protect animals that Mary Connoly could be brought to court. Under the ASPCA anti-cruelty statutes, she was sentenced to a year in jail and Mary Ellen was adopted by "a respectable family." The following year the Society for the Prevention of Cruelty to Children was formed.[10] Who can say what is likely to happen when an environmental bill of rights is established for prisoners covering such items as minimum space requirements, access to fresh air and natural light, recreation and family visits, and access to green spaces. Tenants of public housing projects as well as office and factory workers are going to take a long hard look at their own situations. The associate warden of San Quentin blamed a recent strike on the Church of the New Song; "They have an egalitarian creed and a lot of verbiage which makes them appear to have the same kind of structure as a legitimate religion. The whole thrust is to improve prison conditions, but I think it goes beyond that to making prisons nice places to be." [11]

[10] Clark Wheaton, "What Can You Do About Fifty Million Stray Cats and Dogs?" *Esquire* (March 1973), p. 143.

[11] Sacramento *Bee*, May 2, 1973, p. A2.

4

Hard on the Animals Too

There is more information about the spatial needs of animals in zoos than about human spatial needs. If a zoo animal is given too little, too much, or the wrong kind of space it will become listless, lose its body sheen, fail to reproduce, become sick, and die. Because captive animals, particularly large mammals, are expensive, zoo-keepers have done extensive research on animal spatial needs. Some monkeys are arboreal and need to inhabit the upper reaches of their cages; some rodents will venture into the open only at night, and a hippopotamus will require a wallow pit in which to immerse himself periodically. Hediger concludes that the well-being of the zoo animal is not proportional to the quantity of room at its disposal; it is much more dependent upon the *quality* of the room—that is, on the similarity of the area of landscaping to its territory, the naturalness and the structure of family and social groups, and so forth.[1]

The work of Hediger, Lorenz, Kummer, and other biologists is producing a body of reliable information about the spatial needs of captive animals. Still unanswered, however, is the question of why animals are caged and kept in zoos at all. This question is of more than academic interest and its implications reach beyond the zoo. Just because we know how to keep zoo animals alive, or prisoners alive for that matter, it does not mean that either zoo or prison deserves public support. Both zoo and prison are penultimate hard environments that have done great harm to their inmates. The damage may be easier to observe in captive animals whose natural behavior is also known. The listless caged bear sitting in the corner of the cage watching the visitors or performing tricks for them is not his natural self. Animals that refuse

---

[1] Heini P. Hediger, *Man and Animal in the Zoo* (London: Routledge and Kegan Paul, 1970a), p. 526.

to mate or breed in captivity are not their natural selves. It is fairly easy to document the behavioral anomalies produced by forced confinement in restricted space. Yet the zoo, like the prison, is presumably justified not in terms of its benefits for its inmates but for its benefits to society. No one pretends that animals are benefited from confinement in zoos any more than convicts are benefited from confinement in cells. It is true that some species will gain weight in captivity and live longer than they would in the wild, but the quality of life is so different it is hard to speak of size or longevity as benefits. The zoo is also supposedly justified on the basis of its educational value to society—it helps people to learn what animals look like and something about their behavior. This justification is as questionable as the rehabilitative or even protective value of the prison.

Although some primatologists have been concerned about some of the lessons people have learned by seeing monkeys in zoos, the public education role of the zoo has not received much systematic inquiry. The list of behaviors common in the zoo but relatively uncommon in nature include sexual aberrations, a heavy incidence of aggression, and the blandness of many animals that don't have anything to do in a concrete cage. Although this had led animal biologists to question the research function of the zoo, it has rarely led to significant questions about the zoo's role in public education.

From the descriptive brochures, one receives the impression that the presence of the animals in enclosures is regarded as educational. There is good reason to question the validity of this assumption. Are we trying to teach visitors that a lion can survive in a 15 by 25-foot cage or that occasionally two animals of a threatened species can breed in captivity? The sight of animals waiting for visitors to bring them peanuts would seem to develop a homocentric environmental ethic. One of the most depressing aspects of a zoo visit is the amount of petty sadism and exhibitionism among the visitors, adults as well as children. These unfortunate but all too common occurrences make it evident that the sight of caged animals does not by itself engender respect or learning.

Prior to the development of photography, there was some justification for exhibiting animals as an educational exercise. The zoo provided an opportunity for the public to see what certain animals looked like. However the ready availability of wildlife documentaries showing an animal in its natural habitat as well as the availability of illustrated nature books and magazines compels us to view the problem in a new light. A school teacher or wildlife biologist must ask himself specifically whether he would prefer the public to observe a species in the zoo or see a good documentary film. This question need not be framed in an either/or manner. It may be that certain species can be adequately portrayed in their natural habitat in a large specialized zoo with an adequate staff and budget. Yet other species, particularly large mammals, simply cannot be accommodated in any kind of urban zoo without having gross violence done to their natural behaviors.

Like any hard environment, the zoo is a poor place to undertake research on natural behavior. Heini Hediger, the curator of the Zurich Zoo and probably the foremost student on the behavior of captive animals, states categorically that "the study of the behavior of large animals must be conducted in the wild." [2] Hard and constraining environments leave little room for a full range of behaviors to come into play. For the same reason the zoo is a very poor place for photographing animals. A recent article discusses some of the frustrations of the zoo photographer. The animals sit around almost stuporous and it is hard to find one that is doing anything. As a result some photographers have developed techniques for screening out the steel and concrete environment.

> (The photographer) carefully excludes from her pictures anything that smacks of human manufacture—using selective focus, clever cropping, carefully chosen camera angles, and naturalistic or empty backgrounds. With a 200 mm lens, she finds she can throw some of the zoo hardware so far out of focus it looks like a jungle background . . . Prison bars persist in looking like what they are. However, a concrete wall can be made to look like a section of a cliff face, or shot so far out of focus that it looks like the sky. It is no problem at all to make a hedge with a steel fence in it look like jungle, or a dead tree look alive.[3]

The same techniques can be applied at a prison. A 200 mm lens will photographically transform the convict's cell into a jungle or a park. It is questionable whether this is morally justified or educationally

[2] Heini P. Hediger, "The Development of the Presentation and the Viewing of Animals in Zoological Gardens," in *Development and Evolution of Behavior,* ed. L. R. Aronson *et al.* (San Francisco: W. H. Freeman and Co., 1970b), p. 528.

[3] The Hattersley Class, "Shoot at the Zoo," *Popular Photography,* March, 1972, pp. 96–99.

useful. Photographer Hattersley believed that "successful zoo photography requires persistence, hard work, patience, observation, study, the ability to care, a portrait approach, and knowing how to eliminate the zoo environment from pictures." It would seem more important to eliminate the unnatural conditions in all places of confinement that provoke unnatural responses rather than to develop photographic tricks that convert cages into parks.

The inadequacy of hard institutions for the rehabilitation of inmates and mental patients was discussed in previous chapters. The zoo provides an excellent illustration of the inadequacy of a hard institution as an educational or research resource for the outside society. Unless one's goal is to learn about the effects of confinement, the educational value of the zoo is probably more negative than positive. Despite excellent intentions, it is likely that even the best public zoos are creating stereotypes about animal behavior that are not only incorrect but work against the interests of wildlife preservation.

Any hard institution inevitably distorts behavior. Just as it would be a mistake to confuse the behavior of a captive mammal with the behavior of the same animal in its natural habitat, it would be an even more tragic mistake to confuse the behavior evident in any prison or mental hospital with the "natural" behavior of criminals or mental patients. There is no evidence that most criminals are naturally homosexual in their inclinations even though there is a tremendous incidence of homosexuality inside the walls of any American prison. The apathy and dejected posture characteristic of chronic mental patients is a reflection of the lack of recreational and vocational activities and an inadequate staff-patient ratio. After they've been there a few months, everybody in the mental hospital, staff included, sits around most of the day. When walking, they use a slow institutional gait. A visit to a hard institution will reveal more about the nature of institutional routine than about the behavior of the occupants in their natural environment.

The similarity between the barred doors and barred windows of zoo and prison is obvious. Less apparent but perhaps more fundamental is the similarity between the zoo and mental hospital. In a brilliant paper, Psychiatrist Henri Ellenberger traces the parallel development of the mental hospital and the zoo from being places of public amusement to their present emphasis on humane treatment and public education. The first public mental institution in England, Bethlehem Royal Hospital (later corrupted to Bedlam) was supported by admission fees charged to visitors at the penny gates. Tickets were sold to those members of the public who wanted to view the "antics" of mental patients. The patients would perform in order to receive candy, food, or money. Following the revolution, when the French Government wanted to develop a model zoo, the Natural History Society of Paris appointed a committee of three men to study the project. One of these was Pinel, who had supervised the reform of the Bicêtre Hospital. Out of the efforts of this committee came the *Jardin des Plantes* in Paris, a different sort of zoo which was intended for public education, and which became the model for institutions of its kind during the 19th Century.[4]

A heartening development from every standpoint including that of public education and amusement is the animal park. In a large preserve similar to their natural habitat, water buffalo can wade in swamps and antelope roam the plains. Animals that coexist in nature are placed together, others are separated by concealed moats. Unlike the ordinary zoo in which animals are captive and people roam free, the reverse occurs in the animal park where the people are enclosed in trains and the free-ranging animals move in herds rather than in pairs as they do in most zoos. This reversal of roles has produced some interesting reactions from visitors as well as zoo directors. According to Zoologist Randell Eaton, "Animal parks are better for people, too. In a park the animals wander freely, doing their own thing; you are in the role of trespasser. And in the park, it is the visitors who are cooped up—inside automobiles or monorails—not the animals. You have, incidentally, the sense of being imprisoned—a humbling experience."[5]

The harder the environment, the more the behavior of the occupants will be distorted from its natural state. This has obvious relevance to the zoo where part of its justification is its educational value. The distortions in behavior produced by prisons are less significant as educational failures than as human tragedies. Adjustment to a rigid

[4] Henri F. Ellenberger, "Zoological Garden and Mental Hospital," *Canadian Psychiatric Association Journal*, V (1960), pp. 136–149.

[5] Barbara Ford, "Creature Comforts at the Zoo," *Saturday Review* (August 5, 1972), p. 44.

institutional setting does not guarantee subsequent adjustment after release. If people or animals are to be caged, and we must first question why this should be so, it will be in everyone's interest to see that the conditions are not so unnatural as to twist and deform behavior. This principle is as valid for a worker in a factory and a child in a classroom as it is for a captive animal. Let us use the obvious pathologies of zoo animals to protest the evils of caging human beings, but at the same time let us not overlook the evils of caging animals in unnatural conditions.

The hard zoo consisting of concrete boxes, steel bars, and fixed routine of feeding, watering, and washing by outside maintenance personnel, distorts the behavior of the animals. This distortion reduces the value of the zoo for public education, research, and as a breeding institution to assist endangered species. The *presumed* advantages of the hard zoo all lie in the area of efficiency and maintenance. There is some saving in space and effort if all the cages are lined up in a row so that mass feeding and cleaning techniques can be used. However this overlooks the long-run efficiency of letting the animals look after many of their own needs rather than having an external agency do this. The closer an environment to the animal's natural habitat, the less need there is for the staff to maintain the animals. The high mortality and low breeding rates of many species in hard zoos are other reasons why their presumed efficiency is specious.

I would not want to overdraw the analogy between people in offices, factories, and classrooms on the one hand and caged animals on the other. Thinking by analogy can be helpful but it is necessary to avoid *both* dehumanization and anthropomorphism. The hard zoo can tell us something about the problems of caging large mammals. Perhaps because we are less involved in lions and giraffes than in our own species, the zoo can teach us how to find the proper environment to maintain organisms in natural conditions. If living creatures cannot be left in their original habitat, the least that can be done is to place them in natural and responsive surroundings—natural so that their character is not warped, and responsive so that their individuality and creativity are firmly respected.

5

Funnels and Tunnels:

The Airport as a Place

for People

Airport terminals rank high in any list of socially destructive buildings. They are among the hardest buildings in the land, precast concrete testimonials to the school of monumental architecture. From the exterior most airports are impressive but you wouldn't want to live around one or spend much time inside. Airports are being recognized as a source of air pollution and harmful noise, but I will leave these topics to those more qualified in the natural sciences and concentrate instead on the human environment inside the airport.

Over the years my students and I have observed a number of different airports and interviewed passengers waiting there. This is probably an invalid approach if one considers the airport as a design problem because most airports are not designed for people. They are considered warehouses where the merchandise is sorted and stacked for shipment. No agency or organization feels a responsibility for insuring that waiting time is pleasant or productive. A common misconception is that people spend very little time in airports. This is perhaps true on commuter flights but it hardly applies to cross-country or international flights where flights are delayed, overbooked, consolidated, and cancelled at the slightest pretext. Even if people spent only an hour in the airport per trip, an estimate I believe to be low, there is no reason why this must be wasted time in a cold, sterile, and unfriendly building. Some passengers want to be left alone and their wishes should be respected. The sociofugal layout of airports suits these passengers quite nicely, but the situation is different for passengers who would like to wait in a reassuring and comfortable environment. The terminal atmosphere does nothing to calm people who have latent fears about flying.

I can still remember when flying was fun and airports exciting places to visit. This is hardly the case any longer. The service on a flight to Europe may be as perfunctory as at a Skid Row mission. Edgar Friedenberg observed: "Flights to California have now become sheer anomie— a mélange of drunken salesmen trying to exhibit a rather unconvincing sexual interest in a stewardess who is serving bad but pretentious food whose name she can't pronounce to anxious retired couples on their way to Hawaii and wondering how they can afford it." [1] Passengers filing out to the lobby look weary rather than relieved after such a journey. A TWA official observed:

> Have you ever gone out to Kennedy, stood in the international arrivals building, watched people come through from the customs and whatnot out into the concourse area? Now most of them, like 70 percent of them or so, are people who have just come back from a vacation, and what you should expect to see, I would think, is a uniform array of smiling happy faces, everybody joyous, everybody relaxed, everybody happy, and to be sure, you see quite a few people who obviously have had a hell of a good time. But you see a distressingly large number of people who look harassed and sort of overdone, people who look almost as if they were glad the goddam thing is over.[2]

Since 1948 the air time between New York City and six of the nation's largest cities has been cut about 50 percent. Ground travel time between airport and downtown has increased almost by the same percentage because of the greatly increased traffic congestion. It takes twice as long to get from downtown Manhattan to Kennedy Airport as it does to fly from New York to Washington or New York to Boston. After the arduous trip to the airport, the passenger is left to his own devices and treated as a non-person by all the uniformed personnel chatting with one another. Assuming he finds the right sequence of lines in which to wait and walks down the right tubes, he eventually

---

[1] Edgar Z. Friedenberg, "Campus Community and the Community," *New American Review*, VI (1969), 154.

[2] Horace Sutton and David Butwin, "Will It Be the Soaring Seventies?" *Saturday Review* (January 3, 1970), p. 38.

arrives in a sterile room in which all the black chairs, facing a single direction, are bolted together and he is again ignored by uniformed staff who converse with one another and occasionally make announcements into microphones. When he finally boards the plane by entering a smaller tube and being strapped in a larger one, the uniformed people suddenly become aware of his existence. Coffee, tea, or milk, cocktails, magazines, three-course dinners, films—there is no end to what is done for him. Ignored at the terminal, he reigns as king of the long tube he assumes is on its way across the country. The spatial experience of flying is nil and the social environment is as bad. The stewardess waits on each passenger individually and there is very little possibility for interaction between passengers. Very few passengers have ever made a friend during an air trip.[3] The usual pattern is to mumble some generalities to the passenger sitting in the next seat, perhaps borrow a newspaper if one is especially bold, and say "Excuse me" as one exits to the restroom and returns. Flying in a commercial airline is as desolate an activity as waiting in an air terminal. The person who starts a trip alone will end the trip alone. For the traveling businessman things will not be much better in the plastic motel in the distant city. He will sit alone at a table in the coffee shop of the Holiday Inn reading a newspaper or looking morosely ahead.

Many other buildings we have discussed, such as mental hospitals and jails, also discourage contact between people, but none does this as effectively as the airport. It is a classic example of what psychiatrist Humphry Osmond has called a sociofugal building, in contrast to a sociopetal building, which encourages human contact.[4] The same is true of the prison, which is designed to inhibit interaction but rarely, if ever, does. Prisons are hotbeds of interaction. Civil prisoners as well as POWs have developed elaborate tapping codes that will reach from one isolation cell into another, pass illegal notes (kites) through ventilator shafts, and employ a complex messenger service involving guards as well as inmates. In practice the long corridors and the cold, bare waiting areas of the typical airport are more sociofugal than the isolation wing of the state penitentiary.

[3] Max Jacobson, "Let's Be Seated, More Comfortably," *AIA Journal* (October 1970), p. 74.

[4] "Function as the Basis of Psychiatric Ward Design," *Mental Hospitals*, VIII (1957), 23–29.

Two movies, *The Loved One* and *The Graduate,* have used the Los Angeles Airport to heighten the viewer's sense of loneliness and alienation. At the beginning of *The Graduate,* Dustin Hoffman rides alone and expressionless on an endless belt. The viewer wonders whether the entire film will consist of his silent vigil on the slowly moving conveyer with formless shapes overtaking him on either side. In a cigarette commercial, the announcer describes how people used to feel alone when they smoked a low-nicotine cigarette while the camera travels through the vast empty hollows of an airport building. It seems no accident that an air terminal is used to illustrate how lonely life can be. Crowding doesn't make the terminal any friendlier, because people still remain psychologically apart. Biologist Glen Mc-Bride has studied the way turkeys behave when they are crowded in a coop. Accidental encounters provoked aggression, which destroyed the turkey society, so it is common to find crowded birds lined up at the fence facing outward—eye contact, which would provoke an aggressive response, is thereby minimized.[5] This seems similar to the function of the airport windows, which provide psychological refuge for those who want to avoid potentially unpleasant visual encounters. Passengers can also retreat into newspapers and magazines. There is the apocryphal story of the New York newspaper strike when the seated subway patrons, deprived of their usual refuge in the printed page, unhappily had to meet the eyes of men and women standing above them. Books and magazines mitigate the tension produced by crowding because they allow people to occupy small spaces and refrain from interacting with those in the immediate vicinity.

The present situation is hardest on the elderly, the infirm, families with young children, and gregarious people who like to talk with their neighbors. The lone businessman can easily adapt to the isolating arrangement. Indeed, he may prefer it if he has work to do. However, both children and older people quickly discover that the shiny tile floors are good for sliding, though only the children are pleased at the discovery. If it were not for the presence of anxious adults, for children the airport could be a first-rate play area with its long smooth corridors ideal for running and sliding, its alcoves for hiding, the chairs stacked for climbing, the odd and unrecognizable noises from the pub-

[5] "The Conflict of Crowding," *Discovery* (April 1966), pp. 16–19.

lic address system, and the many doors leading to ramps, hidden stairways, and tunnels.

Rules made by adults discourage children from using the environment creatively. Instead the children (like the adults) are restricted to a few rote responses such as playing the insurance machine, walking up the down escalator, turning on the water fountain, riding the conveyer belt in the baggage section when the attendant isn't present, inspecting the candy machines, checking out the wastebaskets, and pulling the levers on the cigarette machines. Often the airport windows are too high for children to use and parents must lift them in order to watch the planes. However children can still find a lot to do if given half the chance. The exploratory urges of the child propel him to the only flexible, movable, manipulable objects available—and these are likely to be the cigarette machine and the stainless steel ashtray.

If these activities disturb airport managers either on aesthetic or on safety grounds, the most reasonable solution would be to provide opportunities for creative play that don't have hazards. It cannot be denied that children are a legitimate constituency in airport waiting areas. At any time of the day or night one can find children of all ages there. The question of play facilities for children raises the moral question of whether children *should* play in public buildings such as airports. It does not take much observation to see that children already play in airports. Even in dull waiting areas designed solely for adults, children still find things to do. Perhaps it is unnecessary to make special provisions for children in airport terminals because they already have the insurance machines, escalators, and baggage conveyers available to them. The problem is that sooner or later airport rules against children's play will be enforced. The result wil be a lot of frustrated and unhappy children making their parents frustrated and unhappy in turn.

The elderly are also affected by the inflexible and unresponsive interior. A grandmother hears her grandson talking five chairs down the row but she cannot understand what he is saying without access to the facial cues she ordinarily uses. Her sense of separation begins as soon as the family sits down in the institutional row of chairs. Varying the color of the chairs and mounting posters on the walls makes the area prettier, but doesn't help a family of five converse when they have to sit side by side.

It is not that airports are inexpensive or unfurnished, for many are built in the best traditions of monumental sculpture. Rather they seem deliberately designed to eliminate conversation among passengers. The seats are fastened together with armrests, clearly marking off each person's space; the rows are placed back-to-back or arranged classroom style facing the counter where the ticket agent plays the role of teacher. Another assumption is that all people are the same size and shape and therefore all chairs in an area should be identical. To see most waiting rooms, one would never know that coat racks had been invented. A man either wears his coat regardless of the temperature, folds it inelegantly on his lap, or lets it spill over into an adjacent chair. Unless he is fortunate enough to be near a table, parcels either remain on his lap or on the floor while he must stay alert so that others don't trip over them. Two men traveling together will frequently leave an empty seat between them in order to talk without breathing into one another's face. A newspaper, magazine, or briefcase is frequently placed on the empty seat to reserve it. The designers have assumed that air travelers are spectators or misanthropes.

This impersonal institutional atmosphere is due largely to the furnishing of airport waiting areas. Some people come to the airport alone, but a sizable number arrive with family, friends, and business associates. One has only to observe the tightly knit groups that form the moment a plane arrives to realize the potential for social activity in the terminal. The family comes to pick up Billy on furlough or Suzie back from college or Aunt Emmy coming to California for the first time. These are family and friendship groups of the most intense sort. To see them sitting dumbly side by side in the shiny plastic chairs is heartrending. Every so often one family member rises and walks to the water cooler so that he can speak to the rest of the family as he returns to his seat. The start of a conversation is marked by one person leaning forward while the others lean back so that they may at least see one another, but this kind of conversation does not last long. There is no way that two or three people seated side by side can converse comfortably. It is not simply the lack of privacy in the large open spaces, although this is part of it. The main reason is that the chairs are arranged to minimize social intercourse. Most conversations take place between people standing or in clusters where one or two will sit and the rest stand.

Almost every year a bill is introduced into the California legislature to prohibit pay toilets in publicly operated buildings such as airports, and then the bill dies or is defeated. One toilet in each washroom remains free to the public while all others require a coin. Typically the free stall is poorly maintained, lacks a coat rack and door, and not infrequently is out of toilet paper. Without a latch on the inside of the door, the patron is in the awkward position of sitting on the stool while holding the door closed with his foot. A survey of airport patrons by William Polowniak showed that many of them expressed a distaste for pay toilets, especially when children were involved. It was common to find parents suggesting to children that they go under the toilet doors rather than use the coin mechanism. However, the pay toilets are a good source of revenue. In 1969 the pay toilets in the San Francisco International Airport produced a net profit of $48,456—at that time the toilets cost a nickel. In 1970 the user fee was raised to ten cents and the revenue figures have risen accordingly. The situation in the toilets parallels that in the airport waiting areas. The philosophy is to drive people from the free public areas by making them unattractive and uncongenial. Anyone who has had the misfortune to be fogged in and spend the night in an airport knows how bad the sleeping situation is. The armrests on the chairs seem deliberately placed to thwart sleepers. In many airports there are never more than two adjacent seats without an intervening armrest. I doubt if this is done to provide accessible armrests because the person at the end seat still doesn't have one—it is more likely done specifically to discourage passengers from stretching out. Because of the armrest arrangement, most late-night passengers must sleep upright or hunch over in a single seat using an overcoat as a pillow, ignoring the custodian who comes by at regular intervals pushing a pile of mysterious red sawdust with his broom. A ready contrast exists between these rigid chairs and those in the airplane which adjust to reclining positions according to the passenger's convenience. Nowadays, many airports provide, for a fee, special sleeping and dressing rooms in the terminal building or in a special structure close by.

The unresponsiveness of terminal buildings to human intervention became a distinct liability in the aftermath of the bomb scares. The rigid form of the building made it difficult to locate screening devices and guards in any efficient way. The costs of moving walls, changing pathways, or consolidating boarding areas which might have been done economically in a more flexible structure became prohibitive. The result was the cordoning off or "sanitization" of boarding areas for passengers already screened. Family, friends, and well-wishers were denied access to boarding areas. Concessionaires are also being hurt by the security measures. Passengers between flights are not likely to re-enter the main building if they have to be sanitized for a second or third time. The costs of rigid and unresponsive buildings may not be evident until some new need arises.

How is it that a building type that used to be equated with glamor, excitement, and holidays has become a symbol of air and noise pollu-tion as well as isolation, boredom, and dreariness? These are many reasons, including the obvious fact that travel is no longer limited to a few jet-setters, and trips to distant cities for business or pleasure have lost their novelty. Airports are more crowded, lines are longer, it takes more time to get to the airport and almost every airport looks the same. A cartoon shows two passengers meeting and one asking "Where am I?" and the second replying, "I'm not sure! Is this Dallas or Den-ver?" A third man comes up to ask, "Excuse me! Where are we?" and the fourth replies, "Let me see! I think we're either in L.A. or Detroit."

Many of these problems can be attributed to the architectural lay-out and furnishings of the buildings. There is a general unfriendliness produced by the endless corridors, the stark colors, the ubiquitous vending machines, the uncomfortable and cold furniture, and the lack of any warm textures. The word *terminal* means end and in the sense that the building succeeds in ending conversations, it is aptly named. One sees the same vending machines and concessionaires selling the same gewgaws in every city. The restaurant menus are identical, with the same overpriced plastic fare.

The key questions are how things got this way and how they can be changed. Let us begin with the matter of the rows of chairs bolted to-gether. I asked some air terminal people the reasons for this odd arrangement, which none of them would tolerate in their own homes. The answers generally followed a predictable sequence. The first an-swer was that the chairs were bolted together to prevent theft. When I expressed disbelief or laughed, the airport manager would relax and admit this wasn't the real reason, although it is interesting to see how often a security explanation is used to mask economic considerations. It didn't seem likely that people would come all the way out to an airport to steal chairs. For one thing it wasn't clear that anyone wanted these uncomfortable chairs for their own homes. They might be acceptable for an office anteroom or doctor's office, although they are a little cold and stiff for that, and it seemed doubtful that corporation executives and doctors were roaming the countryside stealing chairs. The next reason was that the bolted chairs made it easier for the janitors to sweep. This reason did ring true. With the chairs in straight rows, it was much easier for the janitor to push his broom in an uninterrupted straight line. Janitors have a stake in the buildings they maintain and their interests should be respected in the design process. When a building is designed without thought to maintenance, this is invariably a mistake. However the interests of the custodians must be placed alongside those of the other users of a building. In the airport terminal it would seem that the interests of the janitors had been given excessive weight and those of the passengers too little.

The most significant reason for the antiseptic and sociofugal appearance of airport terminals is indeed an economic one, but not in the sense one might suppose. The present layout and furnishings of the airport are not cheap. They are durable but equally durable items could be more pleasing, comfortable, and sociopetal. In airport economics the largest single source of income comes not from landing fees, but from the concessions, including shops, restaurant, parking garage, insurance counters, and so on. In fact one can see in the waiting areas a conspiracy to drive passengers out to the concessions where they will spend money. Any effort to humanize or provide amenities in the waiting area is a threat to the restaurant, cocktail lounge, newsstand, and gift shop. No one, including the airlines, has a financial stake in the comfort of passengers in the waiting areas. If people spent less money in airport shops, the landing fees for the airlines would be raised. The influence of these commercial interests is seen in the design of the terminal building. A creative proposal for the Houston International Airport called for a system similar to the German airbus, which actually placed the loading or unloading of automobiles within 100 feet of the aircraft. This was discarded because it did not draw the passengers through the various commercial enterprises that pay for the airport.[6]

Passengers have no organization or representation to look after their interests. They are regarded by the airlines as merchandise to be shipped elsewhere and by the concessionaires as sheep to be sheared. Furthermore, those passengers of greatest power and influence have been bought off by the airlines with special lounges and facilities. The super-rich and the powerful (including high government officials) have their own planes and use private airports. The middle-level corporation executive spends his time in the Horizon Club and then in the first-class section of the airplane. All of the amenities are heavily subsidized by the economy class passengers. The extra charge paid by the first-class passengers doesn't come anywhere near reimbursing airlines for providing a first-class section with 50 percent more seating area and probably three times as many stewardesses per actual passenger as in the economy section or the cost of maintaining special "clubs" in airports complete with bartender and bunnies.[7] It can be noted that the furnishings in these airport terminal clubs, which all have conspicuously underdesigned exteriors to minimize the curiosity of the economy passenger who subsidizes them, contain none of the uninteresting and uncomfortable furniture of the plebian waiting areas. These clubs are full of heavy plush chairs and couches, statues and fountains, live green plants and fresh flowers (instead of plastic), as well as free soft drink and coffee service. People who spend time in these lounges have no stake in changing the character of the regular boarding areas.

Some airport furnishings are like school furnishings in that they are *pseudo-fixed* rather than fixed literally. Some of the chairs that are joined together can be taken apart and arranged in a conversational grouping. Even when the chairs are attached to one another permanently, the entire row may be turned around so that at least two rows can face one another rather than all facing in the same direction. I have seen this happen spontaneously only once in what must be hun-

[6] William Cannaday, "Houston International Airport," *Architectural Design* (January 1970), p. 23.

[7] David Sanford, "Come Right in 'Colonel,' 'Admiral,' or Whoever," in *Hot War on the Consumer*, ed. David Sanford et al. (New York: Pitman Publishing Co., 1969), pp. 168–70.

dreds of hours of airport watching. My wife and I have done this ourselves several times and passengers looked at us as if we were crazy. I
have also separated the chairs in pseudo-fixed rows. The results have
been disappointing. Most people are unprepared for the new arrangement and don't know how to use it. In one case I watched in disbelief as
people filed into the rearranged waiting room and returned the chairs
to the straight rows. It was like the old days in the mental hospital
where patients moved the chairs back against the walls "where they
belonged." It is evident that Americans have adapted to the desocial-
izing atmosphere of the airport terminal. This adaptation to withdrawal is the most insidious and frightening aspect of hard architecture.

Things are only going to change when waiting is considered a serious activity instead of dead time of value only to concessionaires.
There is no objection to commercial concessions whether they are public or privately owned—the Mexico City airport with its rows of stalls,
shops, and concessions is an exciting place in which to spend a morning or afternoon. In this kind of space the requirements of a passenger
could go beyond time-filling activities and alcohol-induced indifference. I wait with some anticipation for the first decent airport cinema.
The hackneyed commercial films that pass for airport movies are beyond comment. Passengers will either have to organize or assemble
under the umbrella of a Nader-type organization in order to correct
the inequities of airport terminals where the economy passengers
subsidize the amenities of the first-class passengers. None of this is going
to come about until people begin doing hard time in air terminals—
hard time in the sense of being aware of the specific sources of their
frustrations. Awareness at least provides some hope for corrective action, for considering a humane and comfortable environment as a
right rather than a privilege. Withdrawal is a sure prescription for
even more monumental architecture and sociofugal furnishings.

6

Movable Chairs, Fixed Beliefs, Hard Classrooms[1]

A building can be tight and uncomfortable because people don't know how to use it properly. Fred Steele has developed the idea of *pseudo-fixed space,* or space that seems to be rigid but isn't.[2] Often this rigidity stems from institutional sanctity or the unwillingness of people to deviate from a familiar pattern. In other cases the pseudo-rigidity is produced by the policies of the people responsible for maintaining the space, frequently the janitors or custodians. University classrooms are among the most fixed spaces in the United States today. Elementary school classrooms have loosened up considerably over the last decade and it is common to find innovative arrangements at the primary or secondary levels. Although grade school teachers have been willing to move their desks out among their pupils and teach in teams, professors still insist on lecturing from the front of the room.

In both cavernous lecture halls and small seminar rooms, one is likely to encounter neatly spaced rows of chairs standing at attention before a podium. Occasionally the chairs are bolted in place or hooked together, but usually they are in straight rows. It does not take much imagination to picture students filing in, sitting down, opening notebooks, and sitting mute during the class hour while the instructor stands behind his podium or paces in front of the room. Sanders found teachers and administrators did not often take advantage of innovative

---

[1] Studies were conducted by the writer, Franklin D. Becker, Joan Bee, and Bart Oxley.

[2] Fred I. Steele, "Physical Settings and Organizational Development," in *Social Intervention,* eds. H. A. Hornstein, et al. (New York: Free Press, 1971), 244–54.

furniture arrangements.[3] Portable chairs, he found, rarely were moved from their fixed rows. The sanctity with which straight rows are regarded makes it almost inevitable that departures from them will be considered subversive. Some teachers see the need for guerilla-type rearrangements. One junior high teacher we knew tried for several days to get her students to move their chairs around, but with little success. She finally arrived early one day and rearranged the chairs in a random fashion. When the students arrived, they returned the chairs to their original rows.

Rolfe compared participation in classrooms which had either stationary or movable seating. He concluded that although "the large classrooms with movable seating provided a more comfortable and flexible environment, in which it was easier and more convenient to teach, these rooms did little to change the pattern of teaching or to change the traditional use of space for instruction." [4] A recent study found that the activity patterns in open-plan schools are quite distinct from traditional plan schools. There was less structuring of spaces and teachers were more personal and informal with students. Students worked more often in small groups or alone and used a greater variety of tools.[5] Although educational critics such as Holt[6] and Kohl[7] urge departure from traditional straight-row seating, there has been very little empirical research dealing with this issue. Most experimentation in school architecture, has occurred in the primary schools. One is struck with the physical resemblance between the typical elementary school classroom of twenty years ago and the typical university classroom today. Probably the chief difference is that the university has longer rows and more of them.

Efforts to loosen up the classroom run counter to the security mentality discussed earlier. It may be possible for a teacher to give pupils

[3] D. C. Sanders, *Innovations in Elementary School Classroom Seating*, Bureau of Laboratory Schools Publication No. 10 (Austin: University of Texas, 1958).

[4] Howard C. Rolfe, "Some Observable Differences in Space Use of Learning Situations in Large and Small Classrooms." Ph.D. thesis, University of California at Berkeley, 1961, p. 279.

[5] J. Durlak, B. Beardsley, and J. Murray, "Observation of User Activity Patterns in Open and Traditional Plan School Environments." *Proceedings of the EDRA Conference* (Los Angeles: University of California, 1972), p. 12.4.

[6] John Holt, *How Children Learn* (New York: Pitman Publishing Co., 1967).

[7] Herbert Kohl, *36 Children* (New York: New American Library, 1967).

freedom of space within the room, but students are still forbidden to walk into the halls without a pass. A dedicated teacher might give all pupils passes valid for the entire semester. However, more than hall patrols seem to be in store for urban schools. Many of them reflect advanced stages of the hardening process. Fenced off completely from the community and with only one or two access points, two-way microphones in every classroom, and without outside windows, the dominant themes are isolation and insulation. A welfare mother described her children's school this way:

> The schools are like jails. The classrooms are locked. When the kids are inside, they are locked for "safety." When the kids are outside, they are locked so nobody can steal anything. There are iron gates in the hallway.[8]

The assumption is made that learning can take place best in distraction-free, lockable cells. Human contact in the form of casual conversation ("milling around") is a threat to order and a distraction to the assembly line. The only freedom of space remaining to students and teacher lies within the individual classroom providing they know how to use rooms properly and are willing to do so. In this chapter I would like to discuss the various aspects of classroom layout and utilization. A humane classroom can represent a refuge in a hard building or a base camp out of which efforts to humanize the environment can gradually radiate through the austere hallways, asphalt yards, workshops, and locked offices. Administrators may resist attempts to humanize classrooms on the basis of security considerations. Suggesting that sterile institutional furnishings be replaced with softer and more colorful chairs will produce the objection that nice furnishings will be stolen. At one university I met with students in a dormitory lounge where all the chairs, tables, and ash trays were chained to the floor. It was difficult to show slides because the small table was chained too far away from the wall outlet for the electrical cord to reach. None of the chairs could be moved to a location suitable for viewing the slides. Eventually we balanced the projector precariously on the seat of a chair and everyone sat on the floor. The informality was successful but it seemed wasteful to chain the tables and chairs in this way. Obviously it was not very pleasant or practical for the dormitory residents to use them this

---

[8] Frances Black, "Welfare Mothers," *Ms.* (June 1973), p. 80.

way. Sitting in one of these chairs was like being on a leash. An architecture student in the group mentioned that he was designing a dormitory lounge in which the door would be smaller than the furnishings and all the furniture would be introduced into the room prior to the time the door was completed. Presumably no one would be able to remove the tables and the chairs from the lounge. It isn't too far fetched to assume that people who want to steal these chairs will remove the legs or otherwise abbreviate their size before transporting them out of the room. Perhaps they will steal the furnishings before the door is completed. The hard architecture approach does nothing to deal with the motives of those who steal lounge furniture. In virtually every case I have seen, the theft is not done by outsiders but by the domitory residents themselves who replace the uncomfortable straight-backed chairs in their own rooms with the softer and more comfortable furnishings from the under-utilized lounges. As Van der Ryn and Silverstein, Hsai, and other researchers have found,[9] these formal lounges are designed as status space to impress visiting parents. It is unusual to find a dormitory lounge used to any efficient degree. Lounges are empty most of the time or there are one or two students using it as a study hall. Student interest in preserving the lounge furniture under these conditions is minimal. One can argue that the softer furnishings will be used more efficiently when removed to the students' rooms. However, it would be more sensible to make available softer furnishings for the students' rooms and classrooms (while giving people the option to have hard chairs if they want them) and thereby reduce the motives for removing furnishings from the lounge. One should also attempt to counter the formal atmosphere of dormitory lounges which in spite of the expensive furnishings make them such inhospitable places for students.

STUDY 1: PARTICIPATION

There is no shortage of advocates of the circular or horseshoe seating arrangements. However there is an important difference between ad-

[9] Sim Van der Ryn and M. Silverstein, *Dorms at Berkeley* (Berkeley: Center for Planning and Development Research, 1967). See also Victor Hsai, "Residence Hall Environment," (Master's Thesis, University of Utah, 1967).

vocating a particular kind of seating and demonstrating that it will produce more participation, raise morale, or increase learning in some objective way. On the basis of the many discussions about classroom arrangements, we decided to undertake first a field study of the amount of participation that actually occurred and then secondly a guerrilla-type study in which the arrangements would be altered in a systematic fashion and the effects would be monitored. To avoid creating a bias about what was expected, we decided that we would not inform the instructors whose classrooms would be rearranged.[9]

During the first part of the study we wanted to learn how much participation actually occurred in college classrooms, and whether there was a connection between the size of the class and the amount of participation. This was a naturalitic study, following the methods of Roger Barker[10] and undertaken by six student observers who audited fifty-one classes and unobtrusively recorded how much classroom interaction occurred. If the observer were asked, as occasionally happened in small classes, to identitfy himself, he responded that he had a free hour and just wondered what that particular class was like. This answer seemed to satisfy both students and instructors. To monitor the amount of participation, the observer kept a stopwatch in his pocket or under his jacket and recorded the length of time a student spoke, the number of students who participated, and if possible, whether the discussion involved student and instructor or student and student.

Table 1 shows that class size influenced the amount of student participation. In small classes (6 to 20 students) there was an average of 5.8 minutes of student participation, compared to 2.4 and 2.6 minutes

[9] Prior to the study we gave serious consideration to the ethical aspects of rearranging instructors' rooms without their permission. We reasoned that the rearrangements were a minor inconvenience at most, because it took less than 60 seconds to effect a 100 percent rearrangement of the chairs. Such rearrangements were a naturally occurring phenomenon too, because frequently an instructor would enter a classroom and find the chairs left in an unusual arrangement by the preceding class—e.g. for a discussion or a slide presentation. Finally, we felt that the arrangement of the classroom into straight rows did not stem from a valid transaction between the instructor and the custodian. For years the janitors had been arranging the rooms according to their own expectations and attitudes without consulting the instructors, so for a single class period we arranged it according to ours. No one was greatly inconvenienced, and we believe that something of value was learned from the experience.

[10] *Ecological Psychology* (Stanford: Stanford University Press, 1968).

respectively in medium (21 to 50) and large (50+ students) classes. Statistical analysis showed a reliable difference between the small classes and the large classes, but no difference between the small and medium or the medium and the large classes. Table 2 shows the clear progression in the amount of participation from small to large classes. However, the actual *number* of students participating was roughly similar for small, medium, and large classes. In all cases approximately seven different students participated in some way during the course of the class hour.

TABLE 1

PARTICIPATION TIME IN DIFFERENT-SIZED CLASSES

Class Size	Number of Classes	Av. Total Time of Student Participation	Av. Number of Different Students Participating per Session
Small (6–20)	12	5.8 min.	6.9
Medium (21–50)	12	2.4 min.	6.7
Large (50+)	27	2.6 min.	6.9

TABLE 2

ABOVE AND BELOW MEDIAN CLASSROOM PARTICIPATION

	Small Classes (6–20)	Medium Classes (21–50)	Large Classes (50+)
Above median participation	75%	50%	37%
Below median participation	25%	50%	63%

There is a ready explanation for the seeming paradox that there was more time spent in discussion in small classes, but that approximately the same number of students spoke whether the class was small, medium, or large. In the medium and large classes, the nature of the participation frequently involved requests for clarification or repetition—for example, a student in the back of the room asking that a

The Albuquerque airport is an exception to the generally socio-fugal layout. Chairs are grouped around tables inlaid with brightly colored tiles. The men's restroom has a conversational anteroom, something that is very common in women's restrooms but unheard of in men's.

A private lounge in a Chicago airport; subsidized by economy class passengers but unavailable to them. (at right and below)

Sociofugal furnishings of economy lounges are pseudo-fixed. The cold and impersonal atmosphere inhibits change. This was one of the few occasions when people transformed the straight rows of chairs into a conversational arrangement.

Children can find things to do in airports if given half a chance.

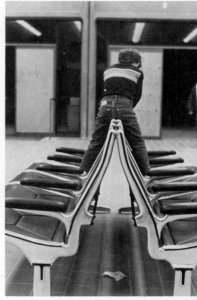

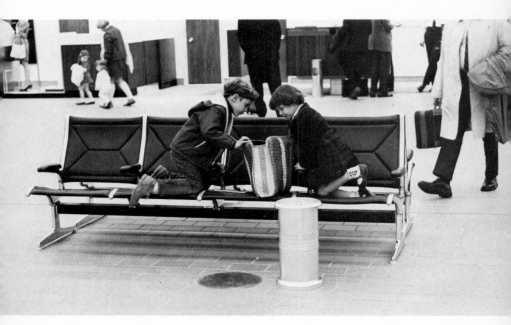

The exterior of this school is a cross between a parking lot and a prison yard. The interior is not much better. Recently school authorities have encouraged art classes to paint murals to brighten up the grounds. The murals have been spared by the graffitists.

Most experimentation with school furnishings has occurred in elementary schools. New college lecture halls still contain rows of chairs bolted to the floor.

Government offices with grey desks, grey file cabinets, walls bare except for clocks and government issue calendars.

Landscaped offices are rated better on attractiveness. There is more privacy for secretaries accustomed to bull pen arrangements but less for executives used to private offices.

Employees considered these windowless offices to be stuffy and uncomfortable. They used green plants and travel posters for psychological escape. Some employers prohibit this kind of personalization.

statement be repeated. This was included by the observers as student participation although it hardly counts as a contribution to intellectual discourse. However, if one looks at the *percentage* of students who participated in each size class, the results parallel those of Barker and Gump, who found that students in small schools participated more on a per capita basis than did students in large schools even though there was a wider range of activities available in the larger school.[11] On a percentage basis, an average of 41 percent participated in small classes, compared to 19 percent and 7 percent in medium and large classes, respectively. It seems clear that there is more time spent in discussion in small classes than in large ones, and a greater proportion of the students is involved in the discussion.

Although the difference between small and large classes is highly reliable from a statistical standpoint, it should be noted that even in the small classes, the total amount of student participation time averages only 12 percent of the class hour.

We turn now to the second phase of the study to learn whether or not a rearrangement of the room would appreciably increase the amount of student participation. In these sessions, the observer arrived at the room just as the previous class was leaving. He then quickly converted the straight rows into a circular arrangement, an operation that took less than 60 seconds. At the time he rearranged the chairs, the observer did not know which particular class would be using the room in the next hour.

The data here were not what we expected. We had hoped to compare participation in the circular arrangement with participation in sessions when the chairs were in straight rows, but in field research one always accepts the possibility that the subjects will exercise options that are unavailable or unlikely in the laboratory. In this case, we found that twenty of the twenty-five classes rearranged the chairs back into straight rows before the class began! This was as true for small classes as it was for larger ones, and for social science classes as well as natural science classes. What was most discouraging was that students were often the instigators in returning to row arrangements, sometimes before the instructor even arrived. In several cases the instructor made negative remarks and the students practically jumped

[11] Roger Barker and Paul Gump, *Big School, Small School* (Stanford: Stanford University Press, 1964).

to rearrange the room according to his wishes. Here are several representative examples from field notes:

> In a physiology class with about 30 chairs which E had arranged into a circle, the first student in the room declared, referring to the room arrangement, "This is weird." Another student said, "It would be great if only 10 or 12 people were in here." A third student said, "Funny classroom." A few minutes later the instructor came in. Sarcastically, the first thing he said was, "Isn't this sweet!" He went on to say, "We'll stop this. I have to have something to hide behind, not like these liberal arts people who can sit around a circle and chat." He moved the desk out further into the room and stood behind it. The chairs were arranged back into rows. He proceeded to lecture for 50 minutes without stopping once. No student said a word the entire time. Twenty-five students were present.

> An education class reflected the students' uneasiness with circular arrangement and their haste in restoring the more familiar pattern. A student entered and said, "Well, what happened?" She walked to the center front and pulled along several chairs and proclaimed "This is the second row." A second student said "This is strange." Another student came in and asked "Are there supposed to be ten chairs in a row?" She counted and rearranged the chairs. The room was back to rows by the time the instructor appeared.

In only one class was there a genuine acceptance of the circular arrangement. In an Integrated Studies class (a new program on the campus) with sixteen students, the teacher responded to the change by saying "Oh, good, we have a different seating arrangement. Did we do this?" The class remained in the circular arrangement and had a relatively high amount of student participation.

STUDY 2: TEACHING LABORATORIES

After finding the meager amount of student participation in traditional classroom settings, we decided to look at various laboratory settings to see if more participation occurred there. We felt that room arrangement, by itself, may be less important than the general manner in which the session is conducted, particularly in terms of the nature of teacher participation and the kinds of activities required of the students.

One observer entered thirteen laboratory sessions of various types. Nine were a variety of physical science laboratories including physics, biology, zoology, botany, and bacteriology. Four were various types of art laboratories: textile design, painting, etc. Laboratories were selected by walking through buildings at different times and selecting the first occupied laboratory. One observer was used because classes were small (9 to 25) and we felt that two strangers in the class would be too obtrusive. In most instances the observer found it advantageous to obtain the consent of the laboratory instructor before recording data. Instructors invariably wanted to know the exact nature of the study. In an attempt to reduce reactivity, instructors were told that a classroom study was being done and that they would be informed about the study after the observation period. In only one case was the observer's presence challenged, when an instructor asked if the observer had departmental permission. This was quickly obtained.

Comparison with unselected control laboratories supports the normality of the observed laboratory sessions. The observer recorded the number and duration of interaction among students (S–S) and students and teacher (S–T). Interaction was defined as a verbal exchange directed to a specific person(s). An interaction was considered terminated when the participants returned to their prior activity or laboratory project. Because of the frequency of interaction among students, the following durational categories were developed to simplify and make more reliable the data collection: 1 = less than 10 seconds, 2 = less than 30 seconds, 3 = more than 30 seconds. The smaller number of student–teacher interactions permitted accurate timing of the duration of the exchange with a stopwatch. The primary reliability safeguard was to devise a simple method of recording data so that complexity and confusion were held to a minimum. Observation periods were 50 minutes, and were randomly selected from each of the three-hour-long laboratory periods to reduce bias from selection of slow first hours or more active second hours.

The observer also recorded the size, arrangement, and level of the class (lower- and upper-division undergraduates), as well as the primary participation pattern of the instructor: walk and comment, lecture, leave, sit and wait. *Walk and comment* referred to an instructor walking around the room and talking with students about their projects and general issues. The instructor was mobile and did not lecture or give a set presentation. *Lecture* referred to the instructor giving a set presentation while remaining at the front of the class. *Leave* referred to the cases where an instructor would give an assignment and then physically leave the setting. *Sit and wait* referred to an instructor who simply sat somewhere in the room and waited for students to come to him or her for advice, help, or instructions.

Results

The contrast between the earlier classroom study and this one was extreme. In general, the laboratory sessions were characterized by their fluidity and the mobility of all the participants. With the exception of one instructor who "sat and waited" and another who lectured, the pattern of instructor participation was "walk and comment." The physical arrangements were impossible to separate into a manageable number of categories. No two labs were alike. In general, the science labs were much more structured than the art labs. Science rooms had long lab tables permanently bolted to the floor while art rooms had movable tables and chairs which changed according to students' needs.

In all laboratories, students were free to come and go as they liked. When a student finished his assignment he left whether or not the scheduled period was over. Art students were assigned projects due on a certain date, and were required only to complete the project by that date. Where, when, and how they worked was their choice. Science students were more dependent on the equipment in the lab for their projects.

Both the total time and the proportion of different students participating were high in the laboratory sessions. On the average, S–T interaction lasted over 12 minutes in each 50-minute observation period, or about 24 percent of the time. This percentage of class time consumed in S–T interaction compares with 12 percent found in regular classrooms in Study I. The more significant fact is that, simultaneous with S–T interaction, interactions were occurring among students throughout the entire period. Study I in orthodox classes found virtually no S–S interaction at all.

Because a general number system was used for recording the duration of S–S interactions, rather than actual time, and many conversations occurred simultaneously, it was not possible to arrive at a figure for the average total minutes of S–S interaction in the laboratory sessions. Instead, the proportion of S–S and S–T interaction that occurred within each time category (less than 10 seconds, 11 to 30 seconds, 31 to 60 seconds plus) were analyzed (see Table 3). Additionally, it was possible with respect to S–T participation to find the range of the durations above 60 seconds and the mean number of seconds of each of these interactions. Table 3 shows that the largest proportion of S–S

TABLE 3

PERCENT STUDENT–STUDENT AND STUDENT–TEACHER INTERACTION
WITHIN 50-MINUTE TIME PERIODS IN LABORATORIES

	Length of Interaction		
	$<$ *10 sec.*	*11–30 sec.*	*31+ sec.*
Student–Student	N = 212	N = 92	N = 96
	53%	23%	24%
Student–Teacher	N = 45	N = 75	N = 99
	20%	34%	45%

$X^2 = 64.46, p < .001$

interactions lasted for less than 10 seconds (53%) with an equal proportion split between 11 to 30 seconds (23%) and 31 to 60 plus seconds (24%). The largest proportion of S–T interactions lasted for 31 or more seconds (average duration of each interaction above 60 seconds was 129 seconds) with the proportion decreasing with shorter interactions.

On the average, over eleven different students, or almost 73 percent of each class, participated in S–S interaction. Over 65 percent of the students participated in S–T interactions. Most students participated in more than one interaction, and with different students at different times. There was no correlation between class size (range from 8 to 25) and percentage of student participation. This is not surprising, given the small size of all the classes in the sample. A larger proportion of different students participated among themselves than with the teacher. Similarly, there was a significantly large number of S–S than S–T interactions.

TABLE 4

AVERAGE NUMBER AND PERCENTAGE OF STUDENT–STUDENT AND
STUDENT–TEACHER PARTICIPATION IN LABORATORY SESSIONS
(13 CLASSES)

	S–S	S–T
Average number of different students participating	11.8	10.5
Average percent of different students participating	73%	65%
Average number of interactions	32.5	20.0
Average number of interactions involving different students	13.0	15.0

STUDY 3: LOCATION AND GRADES

Study 3 was designed to elicit information concerning the relationship between seating position and performance (grades), student's perception of interest in the class, and liking of the teacher as a person.

Earlier studies found that classroom participation varied greatly with seating.[12] More participation occurred toward the front and in the center of the room, indicating increased student involvement as a function of proximity and eye contact with the instructor. It is probable that seating position interacts with other factors to produce the resulting relationships. In other words, sitting in a particular spot may evoke certain role behaviors from the occupant and those around him, but in many cases the person selects a position because it reflects and reinforces goals the person brought with him to the situation. Persons who consider themselves leaders chose to sit at the head rather than side position at rectangular tables.[13]

[12] Robert Sommer, "Classroom Ecology," *Journal of Applied Behavioral Science,* III (1967), 487–503.

[13] F. L. Strodtbeck and L. H. Hook, "The Social Dimensions of a Twelve-Man Jury Table," *Sociometry,* XXIV (1961), 397–415.

Method

The subjects were 282 undergraduate students from three classes at the University of California, Davis. All three classes met in the same room to keep certain aspects of the classroom environment such as size, lighting, and location of the door, constant. Classes with different course topics were selected in order to measure the effect of seating over a more general population than one course topic could offer.

Permission to conduct the study was obtained from each professor. The students were asked on a questionnaire for their sex, class, grade-point average (GPA), and current grade in the class. Students indicated their "liking for the teacher as a person" and the perceived similarity between themselves and the teacher on a 7-point scale. They indicated their position in a row by letter and their seat by number. Students were also asked, "Do you usually sit in this seat or within two seats of it?" Students replying "no" to this last question were eliminated in order to get a more reliable estimate of the proximity effect. Over 70 percent of the students indicated that they usually sat in the same or a nearby seat. Questionnaires were completed during class time and handed to the experimenter, who then left.

Figure I shows grade in the class as a function of seating. Grades decreased as a function of distance away from the instructor both toward the rear and side areas of the room, although the effect of distance was more pronounced in the rear areas. These findings parallel the findings of earlier studies on participation and location in which front–middle locations, where there is the closest proximity and the greatest possibility for eye contact with the teacher, were related to high levels of participation. In the present case, front–middle locations were strongly related to performance, as measured by current grade in the class.

However there was no relationship between overall grade-point average (GPA) and seating position within any single class. This was not surprising to us in view of the restricted range of GPA for these highly selected university students. We were also dealing with large heterogeneous classes from all departments and colleges on the campus. There are large differences between departments and colleges in the kinds of grading used. The last published analysis of local grades showed several departments in which the average student grade was 3.8

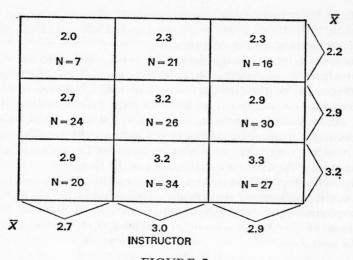

FIGURE I

GRADE IN THE CLASS AS A FUNCTION OF SEATING
(A = 4, B = 3, C = 2)

(on a 4.0 scale), whereas in several other departments, particularly the natural sciences, the average course grade was much lower. It seemed clear that the GPAs of students from these different departments were not directly comparable. The only meaningful comparison would be between examination scores of students enrolled in the same course.

The last part of study 3 was designed to find out about students' perception of other students and the teacher in the classroom. By speaking "about the other" we hoped to get some indication of how their perception of the classroom situation related to seating position, grades, interest, and participation. The study occurred in one of the classes previously used in the seating arrangement–class grade comparison. The 172 students were shown a diagram of the room divided into nine equal sections. Each section was labeled by its position—front, middle, back and left middle, or right. Students were asked to indicate their answers to the following questions on this diagram: "Which section or sections of the room contain students with the most (and then the least) interest in the course?" "Which section or sections contain students with the highest (and lowest) grades?" "In which section or sections in each drawing do you think the teacher thinks the students with the highest (and lowest) grades are?"

Students felt overwhelmingly that the most interested students sat in the front of the class (76 percent of replies) and the least interested ones sat in the rear (92 percent of replies). There is a similar pattern for best and worst grades. Fifty-eight percent replied that the best grades were in the front and 87 percent replied that the worst grades were in the rear. The students thought the teacher perceived the most interested (84 percent of replies) and the students with the best grades (86 percent of replies) sitting in the front.

These findings suggest that the interpretation of more participation and better grades in the front of the room as indicating greater student interest are correct. The data also indicate that students might sit in the front of the room as a means of conveying their interest in a course to the instructor.

STUDY 4: CLASSROOM DECORATIONS

I have also made several attempts to humanize the drab spaces of the college classrooms in which I taught. It may seem odd to anyone unfamiliar with the reality of higher education that I have never taught in a classroom that had even a single picture on the wall. There were no flowers or green things of any kind and no tropical fish, terraria, or tapestry. The classrooms lacked all of those things that would convert a bare room into something lived in. The arguments against decorations are the precepts of hard architecture. One familiar refrain is that decorations would distract people from whatever they are doing. The fact that this principle never prevails at the higher echelons of organization is an interesting paradox. Apparently the work of the school principal or the corporate manager is enhanced by pictures on the wall and plants on the desk while lower-level workers or students would be distracted by the same things. A second argument is based on a nearsighted conception of democracy. If someone were allowed to hang pictures on the wall, somebody else might not like them. What right does person *A* have to impose his taste on person *B*? This argument has been leveled against murals in cafeterias and posters in classrooms. I will readily admit that there is no picture that everyone will find beautiful and stimulating. Yet there are many pictures and murals that will give pleasure to many people and offend no one. There are still others that will give pleasure to a few and offend a few. Finally there are some that will give pleasure to an artist and offend almost everyone else. However a vote against pictures and murals and amenities is at the same time a vote for drabness and sterility. The administrator who believes that someone might complain about a given picture or mural seemingly pays no heed to protest against drab walls and furnishings.

Let me briefly describe one small attempt Linda Davis and I made to improve the decor of a college classroom. Perhaps the only thing unique about the effort is that we systematically attempted to evaulate its effects. Certainly the extent of the decoration was insignificant in relation to the total drabness of the room. The room chosen for decoration was 20 feet by 21 feet, contained twenty-five chairs, and was located in a relatively new classroom building. There were windows along one wall but they did not open and were largely covered by louvers. The room was considered exceptionally barren by the students. The decorations we added included three abstract yarn designs along the back wall, two pictures on the side wall, and two posters at the front. To avoid a confrontation with the administration, nothing was done to deface or alter the room in a major way but rather we simply added some posters, mobiles, and art objects. The two posters were not put in the room by us, but by an anonymous donor. The bulletin board was festooned with flower stickers and a jar of paper flowers was placed on the front table. In the front right corner of the room we hung a blue fish mobile and three Gods-Eyes were placed on the wall above the windows.

Three weeks after the decorating, we conducted a survey among classes meeting in the room. The reactions of students and faculty alike were uniformly positive. Almost everyone liked the decorations when they first saw them and this favorable reaction persisted at least until the time of the survey. The room was now judged to be pleasant, comfortable, cheerful, and relaxing. The students did not feel that the decorations disturbed their concentration during class or hindered it during evening study in the room. Virtually everyone felt that more classrooms on campus should be decorated. Of the four instructors questioned, three were favorable towards the decorations, one said they were messy and somewhat distracting.

The students were also given an opportunity to suggest other improvements. Suggestions included colorfully painted walls, more variety in furnishings, and more windows. It is clear that more than wall decorations are needed to improve classrooms. On the other hand, it is also clear that these decorations did change the appearance of the room in a positive way. The amount of money involved in such decorations is negligible. This would be an excellent opportunity for design classes to get experience in an actual decorating situation that concerns them directly. One cautionary note is needed about the temporary decorations we used. It would be highly advisable that some of the decorations be attached permanently and solidly to the walls. A large number of our decorative items were "borrowed." This included twelve flowers on the bulletin board, one sunset picture, and most of the paper flowers arranged in the bowl. The paper flowers disappeared one by one over weekday nights, while the mobile and Gods-Eyes disappeared over the quarter break. Had the study continued much longer, it is doubtful if any of the decorations would have remained. This is a further argument for using murals and other decorative forms that can be changed but not easily carted away. It is important to avoid decorations being either too fixed or too portable. Some intermediate state is necessary so that things can be altered or removed but not too easily. The security concerns are legitimate but only in the context of the purpose for which the item is intended.

Much of social research is concerned with dispelling myths. I would put many of the attitudes about the distracting or corrupting effects of decorations in the category of myth. There is no proof that spartan surroundings build strength of character. Nor is there any evidence that pictures on the wall, drapes on the windows, or green plants in a classroom will lower student efficiency or classroom performance. It would be nice to lay these superstitions to rest. If somebody wants to argue against amenity on economic grounds, a reasoned discussion can be held on costs, maintenance problems, and so on. In most cases the cost of decorations is so miniscule that this argument quickly vanishes. Most often these economic arguments are screens to cover an almost religious faith in the cleansing properties of hard architecture.

DISCUSSION

The results of the four studies are both depressing and encouraging. Although small classes have more participation than large ones, and this was one of the questions we had originally set out to answer, the difference between them (5.8 minutes versus 2.5 minutes) pales beside the 40+ minutes of class time taken by the instructor. The most encouraging datum for the advocate of small classes is the consistent decrease in the proportion of students participating as class size increases. Although this relationship is hardly surprising (it would be very difficult to imagine half of a class of 100 students participating during a 50-minute hour), it is a genuine phenomenon. The odds of a student participating are much greater in a small class than in a large one.

However, this finding lends little encouragement to the idea that class size is the crucial variable in classroom participation. Cutting a class of 200 students down to 100 probably isn't going to make any difference at all. A reduction from 150 to 20 students is likely, on the basis of our results, to produce an average of 3.3 minutes of additional student participation. It does not seem that reducing class size will by itself accomplish very much if a lecture format is used. This should not be surprising when one considers the actual situation of a classroom inhabited by one teacher who is there to instruct and twenty students who are there to learn. Defining the situation in this manner makes it inevitable that the discussion will flow from one teacher to the students with an occasional request for clarification coming from the students. In all the lecture sessions that were monitored, apart from the laboratories, there was very little student–student interaction.

We were disheartened at the reaction to the guerrilla-type rearrangements. However, we have learned from repeated experience that straight rows are inordinately resistant to change. The customary and expected becomes sacred and any departure from it raises anxiety. We also should not underestimate the security that many faculty and students find in straight-row podium arrangements that make few demands on them for active involvement. The failure of the guerrilla arrangements makes it clear that we should have worked with students and teachers rather than against them. Our initial conception of the research was that students and teachers would respond in a direct way to changed surroundings. Indeed they did, but instead of accepting the new arrangement, they returned things to their original state. Our motives in imposing change from above were not illogical. It would have been difficult and time consuming to request twenty-five instructors and twenty-five classes to try out the new arrangements, i.e. the custodial argument. There was also the risk of a so-called Hawthorne Effect in which a desire to please the experimenter becomes the major consideration.

As events turned out, our model of imposing change from above was deficient. We had assumed that students and teachers would accept an imposed environmental change at least on a trial basis. This model would be appropriate for people with no alternative (i.e. chairs arranged in a circular pattern and bolted to the floor), but not for a low involvement situation where they could easily return to a familiar pattern. Hard architecture works its most insidious effects in the way people adapt to it. Unless one wants to compound withdrawal and alienation, one must work for change with people rather than attempt to change things from above.

The most encouraging finding was the high frequency of participation among all participants in the laboratory sessions. We found that even static and highly structured laboratory environments (desks and tables bolted to the floor) can be surmounted by increased levels of activity by the users. In some cases where the physical environment acts as a barrier to mobility, it may be more realistic to construe the physical environment as accurately reflecting administrative and professional norms against mobility. Providing open classrooms is no guarantee of open education.

The use of any physical environment is jointly determined by the characteristics of the environment and the social structure of those using it. Given an instructor who acts as a resource person and tasks that promote interaction and involvement, some physical arrangements may be easier to use or may more easily facilitate these processes than others. The message of chairs lined up behind each other is that people should not interact with others, but focus interest forward to the instructor (sit and learn). Given an instructor who wanted to move about the classroom acting as a resource person and the encouragement of students to become resources for each other, the typical row arrangement of classrooms could be surmounted. Chairs in a traditional classroom can be rearranged or removed. Yet the difficulty in walking comfortably between the rows and the lack of convenient places against which to lean or sit informally acts as a barrier to interaction. In this sense, the laboratory arrangement makes possible, if not actually facilitating, a high degree of interaction. The long tables, uncomfortable stools, and wide aisles encourage standing, walking, and general movement.

Abstracting from the study of laboratory situations what seem to be essential characteristics of high-interaction situations, one finds: (1) the existence of a specific problem or task that necessitates involvement for its solution; (2) an instructor who allows the assigned task to generate its own questions, which motivates students to find answers to concrete questions; (3) a physical environment that facilitates movement among the participants.

The data on students' perception of interest and their grades as a function of seating position suggest that students select areas of the room according to their desired level of involvement. Large lecture halls facilitate and increase the possibility of students remaining anonymous. Casual comments from students made it clear that sitting close to the professor obliges them out of courtesy to pay attention. This obligation is lessened as distance increases, until finally it is removed entirely. Students in the back feel no obligation to sit erect and pay attention, while it would be a personal affront for those in front not to do so. In the back it may be more impolite to ignore a neighbor speaking at a close distance than to turn attention away from the professor and speak to the neighbor. The salience of the professor's voice is reduced at the rear as classroom noises and conversations compete for attention.

Let me close this chapter with a cautionary note about the limitations of change through physical design. Besides the resistance to be expected from students, administrators, and custodians, there are the very limited returns when no other steps are taken to change the nature of classroom learning.

The crucial question is whether a change in spatial relationships will be accompanied by a change in social relationships. If it isn't, then the spatial change is meaningless and will either be ignored by the students or confuse them to the point of disruption. Flexible classrooms, open classrooms, and laissez-faire classrooms aren't going to make much of a difference unless they parallel a loosening of the social order of the classroom, until they reject the model of the teacher as merely a knowledge source and the students merely as learners. True, students have much to learn from textbooks, experienced adults, and life outside school, but they also have much to teach one another. The open classroom means more than students sitting around in a circle listening to the teacher lecture. I have witnessed college professors lecturing to a class of three graduate students. I have also seen college seminars meeting out of doors on a warm sunny day with the students arranged in straight rows on the lawn. By itself no single change, including carpeting, decorations, portable chairs, reduced class size, or open-air surroundings is going to revolutionize American education, but without these changes no improvement is likely.

7

Alien Buildings

In a bureaucratic building every little thing has a place of its own. The rooms fairly shout—this is where you keep records, this is where you have conferences, this is where you drink coffee, and this is where you see the boss. Every function requires a separate room, which is indicated by another box on the blueprints. The clerk does not enter the executive suite without permission, the accountant has no place in the maintenance area, and the secretary is regarded with puzzled glances and appreciative whistles in the shipping department. The fully developed bureaucratic structure keeps the orbits of people permanently separated. An employee can predict with almost perfect accuracy whom he will meet the entire day. The corollary is that there will be vast numbers of people who work in the same building and never meet. Many people can tolerate this separation with equanimity but I feel frustrated when someone asks me if I know X and all I can say is that he and I have worked in the same building for five years but have never met.

Occasionally something goes wrong and the orbits of people merge. An accident can break the separateness of New York subway riders and get them talking to one another. In an office building a fire alarm, bomb scare, or power failure can bring people together from different floors and status levels. Occasionally a man can meet new people and see new places when he mistakenly emerges from the elevator at the wrong floor. For several years I worked in an office whose location required me to pass a grey door that was always closed. One afternoon I noticed a heavy wire cable protruding from the room like an arm, leaving the door slightly ajar. My curiosity as to whether some machine was trying to escape led me inside, down a narrow staircase, and into a huge windowless area containing massive shielded motors.

Further exploration revealed that the maintenance engineers had offices larger and more lavish than my own, an indication of the relative scale of values in the company.

Another out-of-orbit trip occurred when I found the usual entrance to the public library locked and the sign in the window "Use West Door." Though I am mentally alert generally, I have never known directions. As a boy I imagined that north was up and south was down but I was never sure whether east was to my right or left. The library sign made no sense to me so I entered the first door available, which turned out to be the "south" door. It led through a dim corridor into a brightly lit office area. Clerks on both sides who were busy typing library cards and purchase orders paid no attention to my presence. Further on I found a large storeroom containing unopened crates of books and several shelf areas filled with books that I can only assume were for the use of the library staff. To this day I regret not having examined more closely this librarian's library. The corridor continued past a gay green elevator and a stairway out of *The Hunchback of Notre Dame*. Rather than stray too far from my familiar world, I returned to the main office and asked how to find the stacks. The girl assumed I was library staff and my question had no meaning for her. Suddenly a glint of recognition came into her eyes—I was a user rather than staff! Apparently she hadn't seen a user for years. Because there was no way to pass from the staff area into the user area except by a secret panel in one of the stacks, I returned to the outside the way I entered. I've used the library many times since then but I have never seen another trace of that strange "staff" world.

The segregation of orbits within the building parallels the separation of function of the buildings themselves. As an organization grows, it moves from a separate office to a separate floor to a separate building to a separate campus. Segregation of public building into office complexes or civic centers is the rule. The visitor as well as the state employee is lost in a vast maze of bureaucratic structures. The previous alternative, keeping the buildings scattered throughout different parts of the city and with a style consistent with neighborhood architecture, seemed less efficient to the planners, who equate consolidation with efficiency. In non-owned space, individual territories are actively discouraged, although there may be group territories to intimidate outsiders. A territory is a place that an animal or a person marks out and defends against intruders. Away from his territory an animal is tense, watchful, and fearful. In many species, animals without territories will not mate or reproduce and are more susceptible to predation and disease than animals with places of their own. Among humans, teen-agers as well as salesmen actively defend territories. There are many accounts of gang wars when the members of one gang invade another's "turf." A bureaucratic environment insures that no one can call a space his own. A clerk who occupies the same office for fifteen years is forbidden to bring in a stuffed chair from home (it would look out of place) or place a rug on the bare tile floor (too difficult to keep clean and what about fire insurance?).

Some architects specify in their contracts that the building cannot be altered or changed without their written permission. This includes prohibitions against changing the drapes, moving partitions, or even placing a family portrait on the desk. When the CBS building opened in New York City there was a long list of regulations governing be-havior—people couldn't bring their lunch in or hang anything on the walls or have live flowers or plants on their desk or rearrange their furniture without written permission. The lack of light switches made it difficult to show slides and to disconnect the overhead bulbs, it took two interoffice memos—one to move the chairs and the other to dis-connect the bulbs.[1] It is a characteristic of hard office buildings that no one can control the temperature of their work area and everyone must adapt to the building temperature preferred by the custodian. If there are thermostats scattered throughout the building, they are unadjust-able and clearly labeled "do not touch." Anyone tampering with a local thermostat is likely to throw the whole heating system out of kilter. The most an individual can do to regulate his own environ-ment is tape a piece of cardboard over the air duct. It takes special tools to open the windows and there are apt to be six regulations against it. Even the clocks in the building are beyond local control. Because power failures are a commonplace in most urban areas—brownouts as well as blackouts, and local cutouts for building renova-tion—the clocks always get out of phase. For years I have worked in university buildings where each clock showed a different time. Like the cross-country air traveler, it was not uncommon for a student to

---

[1] Jerome Beatty, "Trade Winds," *Saturday Review* (August 28, 1965), p. 12.

leave one class and arrive in the next one five minutes earlier. A few of these clocks could be adjusted by a tall person on a chair but most are beyond local control. Initially it seemed odd to begin a 9 o'clock lecture with the clock saying 2:30 or 7 o'clock. Anyone connected to his surroundings would feel uncomfortable in this situation. The usual response is to "tune out" the local clock and ignore the messages of one's environment. The problem is more difficult when the local clock is only five or ten minutes off. Then one must question his own timepiece. My own solution is to poll several students sitting in the front row and use the average time of all our watches as mean classroom time (MCT). Situations like this illustrate how people tune out various parts of buildings. Unadjustable clocks, windows that cannot be opened, lights without switches, and unassailable thermostats belong to an environment beyond human control that cannot be changed or altered but only propitiated.

Bureaucratic architecture reaches its acme in institutions for the infirm, handicapped, and elderly. This is no coincidence, because these are places hidden away from public view where the inmates have privileges instead of rights; they are expected to remain passive toward the environment. There are explicit rules, under the guise of protecting public property, against a patient altering his physical surroundings in any way, including the location of the bed he occupies or the drapes on his window. Room arrangements invariably take the form that is easiest to clean and maintain. The drab external appearance of the building is defended on the grounds of economy—it is the best building for the money available. The critic is told "Yes, if we had more money we could have used more color, varied the materials in the surfacing, and added murals, but what we did was the best architectural solution for the money." The most devastating and depressing argument against good design is that the present building was constructed to be in harmony with the already existing (ugly) buildings.

This alien environment is not so much a product of the diabolical conspiracy against individual needs as it is a reflection of a thoughtless and inhumane system of priorities. It will take deliberate planning to construct college dormitories that foster a sense of community, and hospital rooms that make patients feel at ease. Schweitzer's hospital at Lambarene had been criticized as being unhygienic, observations that were confirmed by numerous visitors to the hospital. However, the good doctor wanted to treat the bush people who would be frightened away by a modern hospital maintained according to Western standards. Schweitzer believed that the surroundings should respect the cultural and individual identity of the patient. Although humane buildings may suffer in terms of outward physical beauty and technical efficiency, this is sometimes preferable to making people suffer.

Some spaces are deliberately designed to decrease social contact. An architect designing a library reading room or study hall would be wise to learn the ways in which people use the physical environment to avoid one another. Several studies have shown that freedom from unwanted eye contact is of critical importance in preserving privacy. However, what is being discussed here is not space that is consciously designed to keep people apart, but space that works that way when the goals of the building are otherwise. Architects do not bear the major responsibility for the existence of bureaucratic buildings. Almost by definition these are buildings that belong to no one, not the people who work in them nor those who built them. Their faceless and impersonal style reflects the multicommittee systems under which they were built and a set of regulations designed to insure ease of maintenance. Can a good architect do anything in the face of the increasing bureaucratization of all sectors of society? This is not the loaded question it may seem at first reading. Bureaucracy need not always be used pejoratively because most political scientists consider it the most rational system of administration for a complex society. Max Weber, the father of bureaucratic studies, maintained that a bureaucratic system increased in efficiency to the extent that it *depersonalized* the performance of official tasks. Weber believed "the ideal official conducts his office . . . in a spirit of formalistic impersonality . . . without hatred or passion, and hence without enthusiasm or affection." [2] Note the intimate connection between *official* as a person and a bureaucratic category and *office* as a status and location. In a personal administration where everything comes down from a boss who knows everyone, favors are granted on the basis of whim, fancy, and kinship; in a bureaucratic system, favors can be granted openly only with reference to objective impersonal attributes. But the impersonality that was the antidote to favoritism, nepotism,

[2] "The Essentials of Bureaucratic Organization," *Reader in Bureaucracy*, ed. R. K. Merton et al. (Glencoe: The Free Press, 1952), p. 27.

and arbitrariness, when transferred to the area of design, resulted in faceless buildings in which no one feels at home. There is little the architect can do about the committee system that awards him a contract. Large companies are becoming even larger and corporate clients outnumber individual clients. Undoubtedly the architect has difficulty maintaining an individual style under a committee system whose end product is all too frequently the lowest common denominator of the tastes of everyone involved. There is ample evidence from social-psychological studies that when people come together to discuss topics about which their initial opinions are vague and diffuse, their subsequent opinions will tend to converge toward a common mean. An experienced architect has learned to live with such a system and has developed methods for convincing individual committee members of the virtue of good design. However for an architect to exercise his own personal style does not automatically produce humane architecture. Space that satisfies human needs must take territorial needs into consideration. No matter how well a college dormitory is designed, if the students themselves cannot personalize their rooms they will not feel at home. Impediments to territoriality can be in administrative rules as well as in architecture. However there is an interaction between rules and structure that should be the concern of the architect. A college may prohibit students from hanging up pictures in an effort to save the walls, but if perforated wallboards had been used in the rooms in the first place, the rule would be unnecessary.

To go one step further, provision for group alteration of the environment is necessary for the development of a spirit of community among the residents. Authority over various environmental elements, including such items as washing machines, flower beds, and swimming pools, is vital for the communal spirit. Giving the residents themselves a say in the landscaping through some form of tenant advisory council may result in some unaesthetic arrangements, but the provision for resident-initiated and directed change will permit improvement when things appear unsatisfactory. Such a state of affairs is superior to one in which the environment is fixed permanently at the outset and no change is possible. There must be buildings and rooms that provide occupants with the feeling that they have had some stake in their surroundings and that there is the possibility of altering things when they are unsuitable.

Some corporate headquarters are about as cold and unresponsive as airports. The board room contains a long rectangular table with twelve to twenty chairs on each side and the chairman's place at the head. Everything is dark brown, royal blue, or black to suggest dignity and responsibility. Common sense dictates that meetings in these rooms are largely ceremonial. All the real work of the company is done beforehand. The same ceremonial quality has characterized the various international peace conferences. It is almost unbelievable that the Paris peace conference on Vietnam was delayed for many months because people could not agree on the proper shape for the table. This might have been a reasonable issue had the conference involved a small number of people who would actually be talking together. In point of fact, the large round table was to accommodate more than fifty people in the front row and another fifty behind them. It is not surprising that all the productive arrangements took place in private between Henry Kissinger and Le Duc Tho of North Vietnam.

A designer cannot ignore the symbolic value that some people attach to furniture arrangements. A corporate chairman will insist on the head position at a long rectangular table even though this will place him at an inordinate distance from people at the sides of the table. From the standpoint of maximizing his primary contact area, he would be better off with a side-center chair. Almost invariably the person of the highest status in the room will gravitate to the head position and others will expect him (or her) to occupy it. The expectation that a banquet speaker will occupy the head position is reinforced as much by the attitudes of the audience as of the speaker. The form and organization of a company becomes molded by the pattern of its building. Succeeding generations of corporate officers may wish to change things but they will have to go against the grain of the building.

The hard conference room, like the hard building, is designed to restrict interaction to prescribed patterns. Most often this means statements from the chair followed by brief requests for clarification from the wings and by replies from the chair. Robert's Rules of Order or frequent votes do little to enhance discussion. Except for the person at the head of the table who addresses everyone, the other people talk only to the Chair. At a long conference table, side-by-side interaction would be impolite and distracting. Most votes taken at this kind of meeting are unanimous. Interaction within this type of room can be made polite, superficial, and restricted to prearranged channels. Older hard furniture was wood—stiff and straight-backed. Modern hard furniture is steel, plastic, and glass but still cold, stiff, and unresponsive and if not permanently fixed, at least pseudo-fixed.

LANDSCAPING

Today the hottest issue in office design is office landscaping (*Burolandschaft*). Developed in Germany and brought to this country by the Quickborner team in 1964, landscaping divides spaces with shoulder-level partitions, storage cabinets, and greenery rather than with fixed walls. The basis of office landscaping is fairly complicated and varies from one account to the next.[3] The anticipated gains include improved work efficiency for work teams, increased supervision because people can no longer hide away in private offices, ready identification of bottlenecks and logjams in the form of piled-up papers and lines of people, and reduced costs of renovating. Most of the economies have turned out to be illusory. No one has been able to demonstrate improvements in morale, efficiency, or work habits. Even the logistical aspects of flexibility are inhibited by the pseudo-fixed nature of the partitions and the unwillingness of the social architecture to accommodate structural changes.

Although the open office can be considered as softer architecture than the rabbit warren of private offices, it also has most of the problems connected with openness and flexibility. The few studies of open offices have shown that top management continued to insist upon private offices and ample window space. These people experienced little change with the new arrangement. Secretaries and lower-echelon employees were generally pleased with the landscaping arrangements, which were more colorful and interesting, and contained a lot of greenery. It was the middle-level employees, the supervisors and administrators who previously had closed offices, who keenly resented the loss of privacy in the new arrangement.

Roizen observed that there are rarely more than two status levels in an open area:

[3] Phillip Howard, "Office Landscaping Revisited," *Design and Environment* (Fall 1972), pp. 40–47.

Sitting in a large, open space may permit an employee to see both his immediate superior and his superior's immediate superior. Access to one's boss' boss may cause trouble.[4].

Employees are still able to mark out individual and group territories within the open arrangement. The cues and markers are more subtle— almost invisible to the uninitiated. A boundary marker may be a bank of file cabinets, bookcase, or even a potted plant. Nor do open arrangements dissolve status levels between employees. A person's rank can be readily determined from cues that mean little to an outsider but are easily decipherable by insiders:

> There was no question here about where man's level existed in the organization, where his niche was located. It could be as simple an item as an ashtray. The man with the red ashtray is a senior analyst. The man with the green ashtray is one of our programmers. The ones with two plants next to their desks are supervisors. These things were apparent to everybody, and this satisfied the ego.[5]

Some of the problems with landscaping can be traced to the inadequacy of the social-psychological assumptions used in selling it to clients. Some designers have predicted increases in efficiency and productivity with landscaped offices. This might be successful on an assembly line where work is routinized and productivity is objective, but it is unrealizable in an executive suite where tasks and work styles are unique, and productivity is a nebulous concept at best. An inadequate psychology is also evident in the search for designs that minimize clutter. One justification for office landscaping is that it allows supervisors to see cluttered desks and work stations ladened with piles of paper. Any mess can be quickly investigated and resolved. The psychology of this approach is deficient in two ways. First, a good manager doesn't want to see everything that goes on around him. He knows that when a problem becomes serious it will come to him sooner or later. If he goes out of his way to find problems, he is going to go crazy quickly. Instead he shows executive indifference to minor infractions or peccadillos. Nor is there evidence that a desk laden with papers indi-

---

[4] Ron Roizen, "Office Design and Office Behavior." Unpublished Report, June 17, 1968.

[5] Henry Zenardelli, "A Testimonial to Life in a Landscape," *Office Design*, V (November, 1967), 32.

cates inefficiency. Many productive and creative individuals work in a state of apparent chaos. There are different work styles in every job and profession.

Most American schoolchildren learn to write in a similar way. With standard script tables and penmanship drills, children learn to write at exactly the same angle and use the funny capital Qs and Ds from the charts. Immediately after the penmanship course ends, individual styles develop. With the basic form as guides, people find their own individual writing style—small or large letters, t's crossed high, low, or not at all, wide margins or none, forehand or backhand slant, or vertical letters. The same principle of diversity applies to space use as well. When confronted with a work station, a person will arrange things and use them according to his or her unique needs. One must be intensely skeptical about monistic psychological models of employee performance. Any notion that assumes that people work best standing up, sitting down, or placed side by side or whatever, is psychologically deficient at its core. Any firm will contain introverts, extroverts, cheerleaders, voyeurs, and cave-dwellers.

PERSONALIZATION

There is no single best arrangement of office furniture and no way for a designer, building manager, or psychologist to intuit someone's space needs without meeting the person, seeing the sort of job he or she has to do, and how he or she does it. Every faculty office on my campus comes equipped with a standard complement of furniture—a desk, filing cabinet, table, two or three bookcases, coat rack, and so on. Because all these people have the same job title (professor) and the size and shape of all office pieces are identical, one could conceive of standardized office arrangements. However a walk down the hallways reveals a great diversity of arrangements. One man has placed his bookcase between his desk and the door for maximum privacy. Another has joined together his desk and table to yield a large work area and writing surface as well as considerable distance from any visitor, and a third has placed all furniture against the walls to remove any barriers between himself and the students. Numerous attempts at personalization are evident. Out of their own pocket, faculty purchased rugs, drapes, wall-hangings, and pictures of every description, as well as artifacts and symbols of their respective professions. The same diversity of arrangements is evident in the student dormitories, which also come equipped with a standardized complement of similar furniture. Sometimes I think I have seen every conceivable arrangement of two desks, two beds, two chairs, and two dressers, but invariably I am surprised to find a novel pattern.

Instead of guessing "user needs" one should aim at providing access to a pool or selection of furnishings and allow people to arrange their office areas as they see fit. During the occupation of the administration building during Berkeley's Free Speech Movement crisis in 1964, it was reported that the students had broken into and ransacked the office of President Emeritus Robert Gordon Sproul. When the police had removed the demonstrators, they found Sproul's office in disarray with papers strewn about the floor. The situation was resolved when Sproul's secretary reported that her employer often worked on the floor and left papers strewn about.

The idea that people should be able to control and personalize their work spaces is well within the technical capability of the building industry. It does call for a reversal of the tendency to centralize services and decision-making regarding the physical environment. In the short run it may be cheaper to omit the light switches in an office building, but this makes it difficult to show slides and it is also terribly wasteful of electric power. The same point applies to heating, air conditioning, and humidity controls. There is something tragic about an employee who is officially reprimanded for placing cardboard over her air conditioning vent or a poster on the wall to brighten an otherwise drab office. There is no contradiction between central design and local control provided one develops an overall design scheme that makes allowance for local inputs. One can design a soft building in which each occupant controls his own temperature—hotels and motels do this routinely—or one can design a hard building in which the custodian controls everyone's temperature. In the work on classroom seating described in an earlier chapter, it was found that janitors arranged chairs in accordance with their educational philosophies. They also followed their own standards of temperature, humidity, and illumination. The custodian in my building has a clear conception of where my desk and chair belong. Every morning I move my chair over to the side of the room and every evening he returns it to my desk. He arranges the room according to his scheme and I to mine. Fortunately the rules allow me to move my chair. I visited a conference room in one government agency and found taped to the wall under the President's picture a diagram specifying how every item of furniture in the room was to be arranged.

Pleas for personalizing offices and work spaces are academic and even precious until one sees the drab and impersonal conditions under which many people work. At the offices of a large insurance company I found hundreds of clerk's desks in straight rows in a large open room with phones ringing, people scurrying about, and no one having any control over the thermal, acoustical, or visual environment. A federal agency building is liable to be a maze of offices of identical size, shape, and decor. All the furniture, including desks and bookcases, is government-issue grey and on every wall there is a framed photograph of the President and the agency director. A few executives are able to place maps on the walls for visual relief, but that is all. The quest for stimulating and attractive work places, the right to personalize one's own spaces and control temperature and illumination and noise are not academic issues to people who must spend eight hours a day in these settings. I don't feel it is necessary to "prove" that people in colorful offices will type more accurately, stay healthier, or buy more government bonds than people in drab offices. People should have the right to attractive and humane working conditions. Somehow the onus of the argument for a decent environment always falls upon the person who wants to improve things; the custodians and the rest of the grey wall crowd never have to defend drab and unresponsive buildings. This is a curious double standard. If an employee hangs up a poster by his desk, he is imposing his values and artistic tastes on the other employees, but if the management paints all the walls in the building grey or institutional green, that is part of the natural order. We eventually tune them out and thereby become alienated from the very buildings in which we spend our daylight hours.

Ugly and drab furnishings cannot be justified economically. For a corporation or government agency, colored items would cost only slightly more than grey ones and on a large order the difference would disappear entirely. There is some poetic justice that many of the drab furnishings of state office buildings are manufactured by the state prison system. In private corporations, which buy their furniture in the free market where a wide variety of styles and colors is available, standardization is less a result of economics or efficiency than of insensitivity and deliberate unconcern. There is also more than a hint of authoritarianism in the idea that each employee must accept the specific furniture arrangement provided by the company. In a large corporation or agnecy it would be feasible to give each employee a choice of desk, chair, file cabinet, table, and waste basket from a central furniture pool, not only at the time of employment, but every six months if the person felt like changing things around. This may sound utopian but it isn't. It doesn't take all that long to move furniture. The main objective is not so much to keep the furniture moving as it is to sensitize people to the connection between themselves and their surroundings and counteract the pervasive numbness and apathy. The idea of so many millions of people singlemindedly going to dingy little work stations in large skyscrapers, completely turned off to other people and places, is profoundly disturbing. This kind of numbness to one's surroundings can become a life style.

WINDOWLESS BUILDINGS

Technical and scientific discoveries are responsible for some contemporary architectural forms. The modern egg factory, a long windowless chicken coop, resulted from the discovery that Vitamin D added to the diet of chickens could replace natural daylight. No single breakthrough like this was responsible for the windowless office building. Someone assumed that people didn't "need" natural daylight and no one could prove otherwise. Although the engineering and economic trade-offs of windowless buildings can be clearly specified in terms of heating and cooling efficiency, control over interior illumination, and increased control over access, no one can say for sure what the effects are upon the people confined without natural light. Clinical reactions of claustrophobia are indeed rare but then again phobias as clinical entities are much less common than they used to be. The psychotherapist is now faced with people complaining about alienation and schizoid detachment rather than with fears focused upon a particular object. Environmental damage follows the same model in that the more common variety is the insidious incremental pollutant that rises in amount imperceptibly from one year to the next rather than suddenly and traumatically. Catastrophes such as oil spills still cause a great uproar but apparently more oil gets into the ocean from tankers flushing themselves out and from accumulations of small leaks from refineries, refueling stations, and pleasure boats. The effects of ugly and crowded cities will be seen less in short-run traumatic reactions than in chronic adaptations to noxious conditions.

Windowless buildings may also result from a desire for economy or protection insulation against outside pollutants. A recent study in New York City suggested that the lower stories of some buildings should be sealed because the carbon monoxide levels were almost as high as those on the traffic-laden streets. A continuous monitoring of pollution levels in two Manhattan buildings several miles apart found that federal health standards for carbon monoxide were exceeded inside both buildings. The twenty-story office building in midtown Manhattan had higher levels because the fumes were trapped by surrounding structures. People at the top floors had better air than people lower down but there were still unhealthful amounts of carbon monoxide there also.[6] On my campus there is a policy that air conditioning should be coupled with windowless buildings. The result has been structures that are windowless or contain a series of narrow rectangular slits which provide neither daylight nor a view of the outside. They resemble the openings of a gun tower or army tank. An approach to air pollution that involves sealing buildings and cars seems less effective than dealing directly with the sources of the pollution.

In the course of a design project, I interviewed employees in several underground offices. For them being underground as well as windowless was also a consideration. I was struck by the frequency with which employees hung landscape pictures and posters on the walls. Wild animals, seascapes, forest scenes, and travel posters became surrogate windows. The major complaints concerned the stuffiness and stale air, the lack of change and stimulation, and the unnaturalness of being underground all day. Employees went upstairs at every opportunity except for a few who seemed totally turned off to their surroundings. In addition to the surrogate windows, other psychological escapes were

[6] "Study Suggests Sealing Buildings," Sacramento *Bee*, February 26, 1973, p. A3.

attempted. One man kept a croquet set in his office which he occasionally used in good weather during his lunch hour, others had toy animals on their desks or file cabinets, and few people ever closed their doors. One administrator was asked by his superiors what it would take to induce him to close his door, and he said, "a window in it," so they put windows in all of the doors. He referred to this arrangement as the box within a box.

There are things that can be done to ameliorate working underground. The fundamental question of whether this is desirable at all remains unanswered. Several years ago I was called in by a large insurance company which, for security reasons, wanted to put all its data-processing equipment underground. I was called in to help them determine how to accomplish this at the least psychological cost to the workers. Interestingly enough, the firm's executives were to have offices on the top floors of the building—it was the lower-echelon clerks who would be underground.

To learn what life is like in buildings without windows some employees who worked in another underground data processing firm were questioned:

(Secretary, female) It seems very bright when I go outside. I don't think about being underground much as I have been working in the basement for a long time. I miss the breeze. Plants would be an improvement and more color too. In purchasing we used to call upstairs for a weather report.

(Supervisor, female) I come out like a mole at lunchtime. It is more dull here. Time loses meaning. I have that basement feeling, burrowed in for the day. There is a lack of any buoyancy and change. The work in this particular office is not stimulating, and so things here are depressing. One has to work at maintaining feelings in spite of grey walls and neon lights. I go upstairs to use the bathroom and then I get to look outside.

(Intake desk, female) I lose my sense of time here.

(Intake desk, male) It doesn't bother me except that I get sleepy. I hear others say they feel like moles and want to get outside.

(Intake desk, female) It's terrible. I get depressed and then slap-happy. I eat lunch outside even when it is raining. I get teased about that. I do more gardening. Some people take more work home in order to avoid working here.

(Intake desk, male) I get claustrophobia, I need to get out to see sunshine. I am depressed and go out whenever possible. The basement has the connotation of storage.

(Programmer, male) I was bothered at first, but I am more used to it now. I have been here for six years. No idea of the weather, no idea of what is happening especially regarding light and dark. I feel isolated from the world.

(Programmer, female) The universal opinion is that it is grim. If you put up a picture of the Elysian fields, it would have bars on it. Depressing, confining, irritating, and distracting, especially the air conditioning whine.

(Programmer, female) I can hear the activity but I can't see anyone. It is psychologically upsetting to me and I am going to quit, partly due to the lack of windows. The only way I can tell the weather is if people come in smelly or soaking wet. The poor air circulation and noise, especially in the machine room. All these offices make people bitchy.

(Programmer, female) I am depressed when I get home. I have a much lower efficiency here. Not just the offices, one-person offices are bad. There is a stifling atmosphere, the stagnant air, the noise, the telephones ringing. It is especially bad in winter—it's dark when I come in and dark when I leave.

(Programmer, male) The lack of windows creates more tension. It is relaxing to look out a window for a few seconds. Artificial light, no matter how good, is less good than natural light.

It is only fair to say that we also found underground offices where people were less vehement about their frustrations. Yet no one was enthusiastic about being underground. The most favorable response was tolerance and resignation—"it doesn't bother me anymore." It would be facile and simplistic to equate underground offices with prison cells. Theoretically the office worker has a choice, the prisoner doesn't. Yet the office worker's choice may be more hypothetical than real because in the present instance an increasing number of computers are being located underground for security reasons as well as for better climate control. The workers as extensions of machines follow suit. Discussions

about the free will of architectural consumers are not terribly productive. Theoretically no one *has* to spend time in Kennedy Airport or
Boston City Hall or Joan of Arc Junior High School, but a lot of people do and it is important to know how these buildings affect people.
I am not sure that a free choice model has much validity for civic or
commercial buildings. Much of the time we are trapped in buildings
that do not have our interests at heart and we are oppressed. I would
like to make that oppression conscious so it can be counteracted. The
prisoner who becomes conscious of his oppression will be doing "hard
time." Becoming numb to one's physical and social surroundings is easy
time. In the long run we will only be able to humanize drab and oppressive buildings when more people in hard buildings begin doing
hard time.

In the design project for the insurance company, we made several
suggestions about ways to relieve the dungeonlike quality of the offices.
One recommendation concerned an atrium that would span several
floors and serve as a light well from the upper floors with natural lighting. Research on lighting has shown that office workers greatly over-
estimate the amount of daylight they receive, and they do this in proportion to the distance they are located from the windows.[7] The psychological feeling that one has access to daylight seemed more critical
in many cases than the actual amount of daylight falling on one's desk.
Paneling and the use of textures would be another way to relieve the
basement look. Surrogate windows in the form of tropical fish tanks
or terraria could be provided. Workers could be encouraged to hang
up posters or pictures as well as bring in their own plants and flowers.
Visiting the present corporation offices, I was struck by the contrast
between front areas open to the public, which were colorful and contained oil paintings and mosaics, and the actual office quarters, which
were drab and bare. We also recommended that consideration be given
to exterior greenery.

These are, admittedly, relatively cosmetic changes. Years ago I visited
a women's jail where the warden had painted the bars in pastel colors.
She had also allowed ivy to twine its way up the bars. I still have mixed
feelings about her actions. She did not design her jail nor was she very
happy with it. She softened a hard building as best she could through

---

[7] B. W. P. Wells, "Subjective Responses to the Lighting Installation in a Modern
Office Building and their Design Implications," *Building Science*, 1 (1965), 57–67.

painting and permissive policies. As we have seen, one of the major costs of hard buildings is the difficulty in renovating them to meet changing needs. This warden didn't like her building but when confronted with no other choice she tried to soften it. My first question to the corporation client was whether his company really wanted to put the lower-echelon workers underground. When they felt that this was dictated by security considerations, I could protest, and when that failed either resign or try to soften a hard building. Many other annoyances such as noise, crowding, and poor ventilation are potentiated underground. Complaints are not additive but rather combine in very complex ways—crowding becomes worse because one is underground, and being underground is harder to endure because of the workers' knowledge that the executives have large offices upstairs with splendid views of the city.

🮮🮮🮮

8

Academic Anomie

🮮🮮🮮

Since World War II, universities have received more than their share of monumental buildings. Nowhere is the architecture as hard as on the instant campuses. Planned as a single unit before students and faculty arrive on the scene rather than growing organically one building at a time, the instant campus provides an architect's dream. But although it is visually impressive and monumental in scale and conception, the dream is often flawed in its vision of human psychology and the nature of the educational process. Simon Fraser University, built atop Burnaby Mountain in the best traditions of megastructure, originally had no services or activities available for its occupants—no tawdry gas stations, delicatessens, or bookstores that might distract from the architecture. Eventually the number of people running out of gas or getting flat tires induced the university to permit the construction of a gas station.[1] The paucity of services can be attributed to the idea that students would arrive on campus by bus or car at 9:00 A.M., attend classes until 3:00 and then return home. But higher education on this continent doesn't work that way. A student may have one class at 9:00 A.M. and then another at 1:00 P.M. He may spend some of the intervening hours in the library but most of them sitting around the courtyards and labyrinthine corridors. The University of California at Irvine is another example of monumental architecture with huge concrete structures towering over what was once prime agricultural land. The center of the campus is free of automobiles and bereft of people. It is too large and exposed to provide feelings of privacy or community. The first floor of most buildings is a service level for

---

[1] The gas station outraged architectural critic Ada Louise Huxtable, who called it "a cross between architectural travesty and planning blasphemy" (Vancouver *Sun*, June 30, 1970).

trucks, carts, and machines, a fact that inhibits the development of a pedestrian culture. It is not a campus for walking or meeting people. In the large and empty corridors or out on the deserted center area, meeting another human being is an event. Faculty and students spend as little time as they can in these unfriendly buildings. Only the temporary buildings and the rented trailers seemed pitched at a human scale. A former student described his life on the Irvine Campus:

> It is an eight-hour day, resembling an assembly plant in which the specialist technicians need never make human contact outside the domain of their specialty. Although nicely landscaped, the campus holds no attraction for the students or faculty. I lived in the dorms, which are beautiful, well-appointed housing with sunken living rooms with gas fireplaces, fully carpeted, walnut doors and trim, and suite arrangements which would be very comfortable were it not for the Friday afternoon exodus. In my dorm alone, out of fifty people only two or three would remain on the weekends. After five years there is still not even a beginning sense of community. People resent the factory and only spend the minimum amount of time necessary on campus, preferring to make their homes and community elsewhere. UCI is for punching the time clock.

Attending a conference on one of these cold campuses is an alienating experience. The buildings are never marked and there is no one around to supply directions. Speakers fly in on the morning of their talk, give their lecture, and depart. Nobody stays around to hear anyone else.

The close physical resemblance between campus and prison has prompted Steele Commager to propose an innovative method to handle drug users and at the same time finance universities.[2] Commager suggests that the dormitories should be converted into stalags to accommodate all those students and others convicted of drug offenses and the state would reimburse the universities at the rate of $10,000 per inmate year, a conservative estimate of how much it costs the state to house each prisoner. Although made in jest, the suggestion raises some important questions about the convertibility of hard architecture. Unfortunately, the chances of capitalizing on the physical resemblance of universities and prisons are slight because the cost of remodeling a hard building will probably exceed the cost of building

[2] "Education, Higher," *The New York Times*, March 17, 1973.

a new one. (In the past few years the State of California has closed half of its mental hospitals. It is doubftful if even 10 percent of this space has been converted to productive use. Anachronisms such as San Quentin and Folsom prison are scheduled to be closed and there are no plans for converting them to any other purpose.)

The architect for a 3,000-student junior college in Rhode Island selected a megastructure over a traditional campus plan because he thought a single building would "force disparate groups of students and faculty together." [3] Not only is this a dangerous assumption to make, but it does not even seem to be a winning strategy. Enforced proximity is no guarantee of contact, communication, or community; one must also take into account the functional relationships between the individuals, their motives for coming together, and the amount of space and time provided for informal gatherings.

Crowding by itself does not increase communication or social contact. Indeed it may strengthen a social order that discourages communication in order to prevent overstimulation from too many people in too little space. However, when we talk about high-rise buildings we are probably referring more to *overconcentration* than overcrowding. Although overcrowding refers to an excess of people per square meter, overconcentration refers to an excess of people in one place regardless of size. Two prisoners in a cell may be one too many regardless of cell size, and the same is true of two business women sharing a single executive office where visits from clients and ringing phones disturb the other person no matter how far apart the desks are located. Residents of Park Avenue in New York City below 96th Street are probably not crowded in terms of cubic meters per person, but they are overconcentrated, producing problems in traffic, air quality, noise, and crowds at stores, restaurants, and parks. The residents of Park Avenue above 96th Street, which is the boundary line between the black and white neighborhoods, are both overconcentrated and overcrowded. The concentration of people in urban areas is associated not with a greater sense of community and contact between people but with isolation, loneliness, and crime.

After the disturbances at Columbia University a few years ago, questions were raised about the lack of any academic senate. The adminis-

[3] William Robbins, "Megastructure Will House College for Three Thousand," *The New York Times,* October 27, 1968.

tration opposed the idea, citing the lack of any room on campus large enough to accommodate the entire faculty. The size of classroms also exerts some influence on American higher education. Unlike in primary and secondary education, where there tends to be a standard ratio of teachers and pupils (something like 1 to 25), university classes range from 3 to 1,500 students. Decisions made by a campus architect will influence the ratio of small seminars to middle-sized classes and large lecture sections.

Very little attention has in fact been given to the effect of the vertical campus on the lives of students, faculty, and administrators. Highrise buildings have created enormous concentrations of students, teachers, and clerks, but there is no indication that this has increased contact, communication, or community. Wilensky studied the effects of a new large headquarters building on a trade union. Communication problems arose within the union that had not been there before, as evidenced by this statement of a union official:

> When it was small, we were involved in everything. . . . Now you can't possibly know everything that is going on—just the physical arrangement alone would prevent this. We have a standard joke around here— when we were in the small building, you met the top officials in the john and could learn what was going on. Now we have a john on each floor.[4]

Several years ago I was asked to look at the plans for a new psychology building at a large university. All the animal laboratories were exactly the same size, even though some were designed to accommodate monkeys and others rats and quail. Because I knew that these animals have different spatial requirements, I questioned the reason for the standardized dimensions. The answer of course was that it would not be expedient to give one person less lab space then someone else of equivalent rank. A far more insidious aspect of the building plans was the omission of any room large enough to accommodate all the faculty, much less the graduate students. The chairman admitted that he didn't like department meetings because of the acrimony they had generated in the past. Yet this seemed to assure prescription for alienation, anomie, and the reinforcement of the individual entrepreneur model for faculty.

[4] H. L. Wilensky, "The Trade Union as a Bureaucracy," in *Complex Organizations*, ed. A. Etzioni (New York: Holt, Rinehart and Winston, Inc., 1961), p. 224.

A further change in campus architecture has been the shift away from generalized buildings containing a variety of offices, classrooms, and administrative offices, toward specialized structures designed for a single activity. There were many reasons behind the change to specialized buildings. For one thing it seemed more economical and efficient; a structure devoted entirely to science laboratories could contain extensive facilities for distilled water, oxygen, and the accoutrements of modern science which might then be omitted from structures intended for offices or seminar rooms. Buildings designed solely for faculty offices would not require the large corridors and extensive soundproofing necessary for a classroom structure. The trade-offs involved in specialized buildings have never been seriously analyzed. They do in fact separate the orbits of various constituents. Faculty will talk only with faculty, students will rarely talk with anyone over thirty, and administrators become incestuous. The classroom buildings become student ghettos, with faculty appearing on schedule to give lectures and then departing the moment the class ends. The faculty office buildings become enclaves of middle-aged men and women, and the separation of laboratories and offices places faculty members in a conflict situation.

On a campus where research is more valued than teaching, faculty members will spend more time in the laboratory than in the office. However, a supposed benefit of specialized buildings is that it brings the occupants together. Placing people from biochemistry, English, and geology in the same structure is supposed to facilitate communication, interdisciplinary research, and foster a sense of academic community. To test this assumption, Marina Estabrook and I examined the social relationships in two academic office buildings, the first a nine-story university building containing 98 faculty offices, the second a modest three-story structure containing 117 faculty offices.[5]

We wanted to learn how the form and layout of the building affected contact between people. Other studies had shown that the location within a housing project or tract development affected the amount and kind of neighboring. It seemed that the same consideration would apply in an office building. We started out using virtually the lowest

---

[5] "Social Rank and Acquaintanceship in Two Academic Buildings," in *Comparative Studies in Organizational Behavior*, eds. W. K. Graham and K. H. Roberts (New York: Holt, Rinehart and Winston, 1972).

common denominator of contact, which was the spontaneous recall of the names of other people in the building. Although knowledge of another person's name doesn't guarantee interaction, *not* knowing someone's name under conditions of sharing offices in the same building where name plates are prominently displayed outside each doorway seemed a good index of non-contact. We also asked about the people with whom the individual had coffee (tea or milk) the previous morning or afternoon.

In the nine-story structure we found that the lower a person's academic rank, the fewer people he knew. Assistant professors and lecturers could identify only an average of six people by name, while associate and full professors knew an average of fourteen people. To be known by others was also a function of rank. Full professors were known by an average of 7 people, associate professors by 4, assistant professors by 2.7, and lectures by 2.1 people. Forty-two percent of the respondents took no coffee break the previous morning, another 42 percent drank coffee alone in their office, while 16 percent drank it in the company of others, usually with someone from the same department in one of their offices or in the room where the coffee pot was located. Virtually no faculty had coffee with a student or administrator. Faculty opinions on the architecture of the building, were solicited and then rated along a five-point scale:

very favorable	1	respondent
mildly favorable	5	"
neutral	15	"
mildly unfavorable	14	"
very unfavorable	15	"

The unpleasant comments referred to the building as cold, stiff, impersonal, drab, and unimaginative. The few positive comments indicated that the building was conceived as practical and functional. We did not know how to score the comment of one professor who stated that the building was "on a par with the school."

There is no formal feedback procedure for complaints about a building. Authority is so remote that all one sees are one's colleagues and students, and perhaps the custodian. The administration is not likely to take complaints very seriously. As one campus architect put it,

"There is no point in getting excited about complaints. Whenever you open a new building, there are complaints but they die down in six months. "From the occupant's standpoint, if six months of complaints don't produce any results, there is probably not too much point in continuing to complain.

In colleges in which there is a department of design and/or architecture, there is usually an enormous chasm between it and the people responsible for designing and maintaining the campus. When we interviewed faculty in a department of landscape architecture regarding outdoor study spaces on their campus, the most common reply was, "This isn't our responsibility, it belongs to Buildings and Grounds." Few architecture faculty feel personally responsible for campus buildings. This too is the result of the administrative process, from which they are usually excluded. Design students have little influence in the selection or layout of furnishings. The outcome is predictable, particularly if one realizes that furnishings are often selected by a business agent out of a catalogue supplied by the state prison system.

The second study took place in a three-story academic building constructed around a courtyard which was never used because it provided no privacy. Our sample consisted of 80 of the 117 faculty in the building: 44 percent of the full professors, 54 percent of the associate professors, and 80 percent of the assistant professors and lecturers, respectively. The figures reflect a decreasing proportion of people in the higher status levels because of the difficulty in tracking them down. Repeated visits and phone calls were able to turn up only a bare majority of full professors. There seems a clear relationship between accessibility and academic rank. Lower-ranking faculty spend more time in their offices with their doors open than do higher-ranking faculty.

We also asked about the length of time that the respondents had been on campus. We were able therefore to compare notability (being known by others) with length of time of employment on campus as well as with academic rank. Full professors were known by an average of 10 people, associate professors by 9, assistant professors by 7.6, and lecturers by 3 people. We then performed a detailed statistical analysis to remove the confounding between rank and length of employment. Basically, when the effects of rank are removed (through partial correlations), the relationship between length of employment and notability disappears, while if one removes length of employment from the rank-notability relationship, the correlation is low but still reliable. One may conclude from this analysis that both knowing others and being known are primarily functions of rank and next of length of employment within ranks. People in departments who shared space on the same floor were better acquainted than people in departments on different floors. Also, departments whose interests and activities brought them together tended to know one another—for example, the faculty in economics and agricultural economics were acquainted even though they were situated on different floors.

The lack of lounge areas or any common spaces where people could come together for informal contacts exerted a significant effect on social relationships in the building. More than two-thirds of the faculty had not had coffee the preceding morning (or afternoon) or had it alone in their offices. Fewer than 1 in 20 faculty had coffee (or another beverage) with a student that day, and none had coffee with on administrator. Most of those who shared their coffee breaks with colleagues were tenured faculty. There were 19 full or associate professors who shared coffee breaks, compared to only 7 assistant professors or lecturers. Tenured faculty drank coffee with tenured faculty and only 1 of the 19 had coffee with a nontenured person. All 6 assistant professors who shared a coffee break took coffee with another of the nontenured faculty. Nine secretaries in this building were also asked about their coffee breaks. The same trend toward segregation by status was evident. Five secretaries had taken coffee with other secretaries, 3 drank alone, and 1 had no coffee. A group of 14 administrators from various campus facilities was asked about their coffee-drinking habits. These people had coffee with an aggregate of 30 individuals but not one of these was a faculty member or student.

It seems reasonable to conclude that some of this isolation between students, faculty, and administrators, as well as between individual faculty members, is a result of campus architecture. Placing administrators in a separate building on a distant part of the campus cannot help but reduce contact with faculty and students. The administration's explicit policies prohibiting social lounges in academic buildings also reduces contact among members of the faculty. The policy is a logical outgrowth of the idea that specialization means efficiency and economy. Rather than putting social lounges in academic buildings, they would be placed in separate social buildings (cafeterias, student unions, or the faculty club). Because most faculty like to drink their coffee close to where they work rather than walk across campus for it, the result is that these public lounges are underused and most faculty drink their coffee alone or go without.

A further issue in campus architecture is the relationship between private offices and the highly individualistic mode of American higher education. The description of faculty as "a band of entrepreneurs" fits almost every university on the continent. Even though this is probably connected to the private office syndrome, it would be simplistic to suggest that placing two faculty in an office would increase communication. The result of placing two faculty in a single office would be a system of time-sharing in which one person arranges to be out while the other person sees students or has office hours. As we saw in open-plan offices, there would be spatial markers to keep territories separate. Mary's desk and file cabinet and chair would be on one side of the dividing line, Bill's desk, file cabinet, and visitor's chair would be on the other side of the dividing line. Visitors would quickly sense on which side of the room they belonged and scrupulously avoid the other occupant's territory. Essentially we would have two unsatisfactory private offices in a single cell and social barriers would replace the wall.

This does not seem a logical route to academic community. In a rewards system based on individual achievement, double offices are only going to make people unhappy. There may be some resultant economies for the institution, but it is doubtful whether or not these outweigh lowered morale among occupants. Faculty employ two devices to deal with overconcentrated offices—avoidance of the office as a work place and a rigid spatial order within the room. Because they can (and do) avoid their office entirely, unlike the confined prisoner or zoo animal, the effects of overconcentration will be revealed less in individal pathology than in a loss of academic community.

░░░

9

Awards and

Social Responsibility[1]

░░░

All professions have their myths, complete with devils, heroes, and homunculi. The architect's devils are the bankers and corporation executives who want buildings constructed according to a ledger sheet, schlock builders creating subdivisions on the backs of envelopes, and a public that does not know how to appreciate the subtleties of fine architecture. The heroes are those few individuals able to triumph over the devils and create strong, bold, and impressive buildings. All too often these are hard monumental buildings as well. Architectural prizes and criticism have fostered a star system by emphasizing novelty and private expression as major design values. By its nature this system does not consistently encourage architecture designed to "fit in" but rather work that "stands out." [2] A main category of prize-winners are the escape places—the vacation homes nestled in the mountains or on the vanishing coastline.

In architecture as in many other fields, awards are reserved for those who work outside the mainstream and thus are not likely to be honored by the elective process. Awards are a method by which a profession can encourage innovation and creativity among its members without any implication about the popular appeal of the work. Often the basis of the award is the presumed *lack* of popular appeal of the individual's contribution. If a work possessed popular appeal and was

---

[1] A shortened version of this chapter appeared in the May 1973 issue of the *A.I.A. Journal*. I am grateful to Steele Wotkyns and Arthur Allen for their thoughtful comments.

[2] Francis D. Lethbridge, "The Honors Awards Program in Retrospect," *A.I.A. Journal* (May 1973), p. 22.

acclaimed by the media, it would be redundant for a profession to create a separate apparatus for bestowing awards upon it.

In many fields, awards based on private and esoteric criteria may appear to represent public acclaim. Because the public cannot be expected to understand the work at the frontiers of knowledge, a board of competent specialists *acting in the public's name* awards prizes. The phrasing of such awards explicitly mentions service to humanity. There is an inherent ambiguity in all instances where the criteria for the award are esoteric but the award itself is made in the public's name and becomes a media event.

The often antipublic bias of professional awards committees is disturbing. In architects such a bias may result in a contemptuous attitude toward the very people who will occupy the architect-designed buildings. People are told "you should like that building because it is great architecture" just as a child is told "you should eat your chicken soup because it is good for you." The designer's authority rather than responsibility is the basis of such an attitude, often expressed as an esthetic value—that the goal of the architect is to create beautiful buildings. This can constitute a specific rejection of the designer's responsibility to a building's occupants. A poster celebrating Paul Rudolph's Art Architecture Building at Yale describes how the building "burnt, closed, walled off, in tumult, carried a legacy of confusion and overwhelming sadness during the two-year restoration process. But not even the holocaust of fire could in any ultimate way tear the heart from this monument of American architecture, this presence on the Yale Campus." After discussing the building's terrifying, ferocious nobility, the poster concedes:

> It is, perhaps for these reasons, not an easy building to live with. Physically it is often uncomfortable. It gets hot when the sun pours in. Security controls are difficult. Offices are cramped. The spaces are not perfect for twenty-foot high paintings or intimate conversation or classroom study. The lighting is inadequate. There are great difficulties in manipulating one's personal environment.[3]

It is difficult to understand how a building that made so many people so uncomfortable that some even tried to burn it down could merit a citation for good design. An awards system so unconcerned

---

[3] Henry Wollman, "Calendar for the Yale School of Architecture," 1971.

with the responses of architecture students and faculty is not likely to heed the responses of prisoners to their cells or workers to their offices and factories. Professional disinterest in popular tastes is a dangerous trend for a democracy. Hard buildings often possess a monumental quality that makes them look as if they were created for some contest. About all you can do with the cold brutal edifice is give it some kind of award. You can't live in it or work there. The idea that people should "live up to buildings" implies that they should change their behavior to fit the architecture. This notion is only appropriate for a building, such as a cathedral, where there is a clear agreement among the designer, client, and consumer about behaviors to be expected in the particular setting and the attitudes to be engendered.

Problems arise when one group of people (clients) accept esoteric standards for buildings that will accommodate others (consumers) who lack any voice in design decisions. One hundred years ago when great stone monuments with turrets and cupolas were in fashion, some prisons and jails were hailed as examples of fine architecture. Now the plaudits go to modern "correctional institutions" that blend in with their surroundings because the security aspects are unobtrusive. Although the older prisons of this country may indeed be splendid examples of monumental architecture, they should be tourist attractions or architectural museums rather than places where men and women spend years without adequate space, sunlight, heating, ventilation, and recreation. The system of architectural awards neither created nor perpetuates the prison, but *to the extent that it encourages professional disinterest in popular response to buildings and favors monumental structures, it provides support for hard architecture.* Once the principle is accepted that monumental buildings are acceptable for college students and office workers who must "live up" to an environment that oppresses them, it is difficult to question the predicament of prison inmates. Any oppressive situation tolerated in society is inevitably used to justify other oppressions.

ARCHITECTURAL CRITICISM

Architectural criticism has also neglected the social responsibilities of the design professions. Focused upon novelty, private expression, and cute phrases, such criticism, like the awards system, fosters a star system that is constantly recounting what the beautiful people are doing. It would be a mistake to exaggerate the importance of architectural criticism in determining what is built or why. Most of what is said in this section concerns the *potential* of architectural criticism rather than its present state. Very few non-architects have read even a single piece of architectural criticism. Only a minority of newspapers carry it and then only in a single weekly column buried in a back section. The same lack of interest is found in television and national magazines. Architectural criticism has no following because it ignores those features of buildings, neighborhoods, and cities that concern most people. Critics are not interested in vernacular buildings—the places where most people live and work, including restaurants, bowling alleys, and gas stations. Most critics would describe these as non-architecture or just plain buildings.

Although this approach may be valid in the fine arts, it is out of place in an applied art such as architecture or interior design. The former drama critic for *The New York Times,* Stanley Kauffman, saw his work as very different from that of the journalist whose task it was to interpret popular culture: "Since art critics do not review billboards, music critics do not review dance bands and pop singers, why should a drama critic review *Cactus Flower?*" [4] He did not see his job as interpreting other people's responses to plays, but rather to report upon his own sensitive and intuitive reaction to a play. "The only way the critic can be of service to his readers," he wrote, "is by providing his own standards—with his own insights and defects—as a frame of reference." Whether or not people like a show or a building is not terribly important to a fine arts critic. Nor is he concerned with telling other people whether *they* would like something, only whether he liked it.

Architecture is not a pure art; it is an applied art. The description of buildings as great hollow sculpture ignores their role in providing shelter, amenity, and satisfaction for occupants as well as for visitors, passersby, and neighborhood residents. The sculptural model is valid for true monuments. No one would attempt to evaluate the suitability of the Lincoln Memorial or Grant's Tomb as an office building or

---

[4] "Drama on the Times," *New American Review:* No. 1 (New York: New American Library, 1967), p. 43.

residence. Architectural critics who apply sculptural values to apartment buildings, banks, and airport terminals, however, are off their legitimate turf. If they want to discuss non-monumental buildings, they will have to use a different set of standards which includes the comfort and satisfaction of the occupants and other people concerned with a building.

Unlike the occupants who must live in them, architectural critics have thrived on hard buildings. They have christened the trend toward windowless concrete as the *New Brutalism*. If one applies this phrase to human society, its frightening implications become apparent. But architectural critics laud these concrete monoliths for their honesty and integrity. The bare pipes and exposed wiring courageously portray the guts of the building. It is logical to photograph such buildings without any people around, for a human presence would only detract from the building. A more sophisticated critical view is based upon reflection rather than analogy. Brutal buildings are a response to a brutal society, just as cheap and tawdry buildings reflect the commercialism of American society. Romanticizing one's oppression is a valid coping mechanism provided nothing can be done to relieve it.

As it is practiced today, architectural criticism is based on the responses of educated, cultured, intuitive, and aesthetically sensitive middle-class individuals to monumental buildings. It represents the private experience of the critic and thereby could perhaps qualify as an art form in its own right. A novelist tries to touch impulses and ideas that others can only vaguely sense. The artist puts them on canvas and the sculptor casts them in bronze. Kafka's short stories represent his own private vision rather than the way most people see the world. In the same way, the architectural critic expresses how he or she sees a building and not how other people see it. The problem arises when such criticism is interpreted as reflecting public acceptance of buildings. Substituting the word *monument* every time an architectural critic mentions a specific building type will aid the reader in understanding what the critic is trying to accomplish. It can also help in understanding why critics never include the opinions of occupants toward a given structure. Indeed it is common to find buildings praised or damned before they have been opened to public use.

It requires great sensitivity and talent to translate one's responses to a building (or play or painting) into beautiful prose. When asked for their response to a work of art, most people will shrug or mutter a terse evaluative comment, but will have difficulty supplying specific reasons. I would like to see the critical faculties of people more finely developed. To the extent that critics see education as their task, their efforts are praiseworthy. However critics in the fine arts are, it seems, more interested in reporting their private visions than in raising public consciousness.

Purely functional standards of criticism that would ignore beauty, delight, surprise, and other subjective values are not recommended. Nor is an awards system that simply codifies public tastes. There is no need for architectural critics who serve only as public opinion pollisters. To earn his salary, a good critic must do more than reflect public tastes—he must try to understand these tastes and their origins while attempting to elevate them.

EVALUATION

Awards and "fine arts" type of criticism have encouraged monumental buildings that are often hard and oppressive. They have also neglected the responses of occupants and non-designers. A useful antidote to esoteric standards would be an ongoing program of building evaluation that would include both physical measurements (room temperature, humidity, air flow, lighting, visual and acoustical separation) and subjective estimates (beauty, excitement, variety, and warmth). Evaluation should not be confused with an awards system. It is the responsibility of every professional to evaluate his or her own work. A teacher may do this through class examinations and a surgeon through a physical exam or a post mortem. This evaluation would not be the same as an award given to an outstanding teacher or surgeon by a national society. In general, evaluation tends to be objective, private (in the sense that the results are secured by the professional for private use within the context of a client or consumer relationship), and most of the time will produce ratings in a middle range of achievement. An awards system is necessarily public and favorable to the recipient. Except as a very infrequent type of spoof, there are no awards given for mediocre or poor performance. This point would be too obvious to make, except that it illustrates a major difference between evaluation and awards. Whenever anyone advocates the use of ongoing building evaluation, there are many who interpret this as a proposal for a new type of awards system.

All professions in this country have been loath to subject themselves to outside evaluation. What has evolved instead in law, medicine, engineering, and architecture is a system of professional self-regulation. With lawyers deciding upon the criteria for admission to law school and the bar, as well as shaping school curriculum and holding the keys to law offices, it is not surprising that the bar should become private in its professional discourse. One can see the same trends in virtually every other profession. It is not my intention to criticize this state of affairs but only to show its role in shaping a private awards system that appears to resemble public acclaim but is not the same. I don't know of a single profession in which professional awards could reasonably be considered to reflect public acclaim. If the two are related at all, it is because the award catches the attention of the media and the recipient becomes a public figure. The Nobel Prize for chemistry is not a mark of public acclaim but it will bring public acclaim. This has led me to a greater respect for the rationale and potential of a professional awards system, providing one understands its nature. It is a method by which a profession presents a public image. If such a system is allowed to fall into mutual back-patting and self-congratulation, the fault lies with the committees in charge rather than with the system as such. The awards system is one among many of raising the public consciousness about architecture. There is a tremendous amount of work needed if the wave of urban blight is to be halted and reversed.

At the present time most architectural awards are made for technical virtuosity and aesthetic talent. Some of these awards are made by trade associations such as the Precast Concrete Institute or the Institute of Steel Construction, which place heavy emphasis on the use of particular materials. In such cases no functional evaluation of the building is made. The much-vaunted Breakthrough program sponsored by the Department of Housing and Urban Development (HUD) was intended to develop new materials and methods in home construction. Those architects and builders who were able to overcome the red tape and bureaucratic inertia produced housing units in several parts of the country which were well publicized by HUD on the basis of visual appearance and the use of innovative construction methods. However, nothing was ever said about the reactions of the tenants to the Breakthrough units.[5] My hunch is that this omission of user response will eventually be remedied in the form of tenant surveys, but this kind of post-mortem does not feed forward to future construction. The Breakthrough projects are completed and there are no plans to conduct a new competition for additional system or prototypes. This disinterest in evaluation is typical of HUD:

> Success for the department responsible for building new housing is measured by *how many new* units are built each year and not by what kind of units, how much they will cost to maintain, how long they will last, or how satisfactory a living environment they will provide.[6]

It is necessary to encourage the use of new materials and construction methods in the housing industry as long as they provide good housing for the occupants. Innovations must be more than unique or new; they must be addressed to important human concerns rather than the self-indulgence of the designer, client, profession, or government agency. Building evaluation is not a new kind of awards system. Rather it is an ongoing process within a programming-design-construction-evaluation-redesign cycle. As I have discussed elsewhere, there should be no design without evaluation, and no evaluation without redesign.[7]

Architectural awards can help to raise public consciousness about buildings if they are used properly. Whether they are to be more than fashion shows is a matter for the architectural profession to decide. I would offer two specific suggestions for making the awards system more responsive to user needs:

1. No building shell be nominated for an award until it has been open and in use for at least twelve months.

2. Some effort shall be made to systematically obtain and include the opinions of the building's occupants in the decision process.

Neither of these recommendations precludes the use of engineering, aesthetics, or any other relevant criteria of good design. All they do is add user satisfaction to the list. One would not give an award to

[5] U.S. Department of Housing and Urban Development, *Operation: Breakthrough,* 1972.

[6] Oscar Newman, *Defensible Space* (New York: The Macmillan Co., 1972), p. 188.

[7] Robert Sommer, *Design Awareness* (San Francisco: Rinehart Press, 1972).

an airplane without knowing how well it flies or a ship without knowing its sailing capabilities, and one should not give an award to a building without knowing how well it provides shelter and amenity for its occupants.

At the present time most jurors in design competitions base their decisions on photographs and brochures. This tends to overemphasize visual factors at the expense of the other sense modalities, including hearing, touch, and the sense of movement through a building. One juror expressed his frustration with this procedure:

> Studying photographs, plans, and verbal descriptions of a project amounts to a two-dimensional examination of a three-dimensional project. Although it may be true that the camera never lies, it is just as true that the beguiling photograph can obscure a host of shortcomings. Jurors try to see through this as well as they can, but there is always the danger of being seduced by an expertly contrived two-dimensional image.[8]

Most design competitions still rely on photographs and brochures, but the national awards program of the American Institute of Architects does require that at least one member of the jury shall have seen the building being considered. I would extend this requirement to having the juror make some systematic effort to secure occupant response to the building (more than "everybody looked pleased with the building as I walked through it") and present this information to the other panel members.

[8] Vincent G. Kling, "Confessions of an Awards Juror," *A.I.A. Journal* (May 1973), p. 27.

Epilogue:

The Horse Inside the Cart

Graffiti in the New York subways are considered more of a problem than the depressing and squalid environment. Cat faces painted along the Los Angeles River channel are of more concern to the City Council than the concrete embankment, the power lines, and the endless fences. The trade-offs in what we are presently doing are often not apparent until some dramatic event or change occurs—hence the need for soft buildings that encourage experimentation or, at least, can accommodate change. Soft buildings will require a new collaboration between designers and the public. After he designed a hard building, it was easy for an architect to walk away and collect his prizes. There wasn't much he or anyone else could do about changing the place, because renovations were costly. A soft building places more responsibility on the designer to help occupants get their money's worth—he should assist them in using it wisely and creatively, and be able to adapt it to changing needs. It is a mistake to provide responsive spaces when people don't know how to use them. The school system developed by the School Construction System Development team in California was intended to provide an educational setting of maximum flexibility. After the system had been operating for several years, one of the original designers went back and evaluated the schools. He found that a majority of teachers were not aware of a flexibility inherent in the buildings and others, and others were only moderately aware that things could be moved around, and did not know how to do it. Only 23 percent of the teachers in the ten schools evaluated had been involved in some alteration to their teaching space which required a physical change in the building.[1] Passivity regarding the physical environment must be counteracted if people are going to use the flexibility made possible by new materials and technologies.

I am not advocating a new style of Sociable Architecture. Not every airline passenger wants to converse with other people. Some do, and there should be good social spaces for them, but the solitary traveler who wants to work by himself should have sociofugal space. Nor do I believe that every employee works best in an open office. I do my best thinking in the living room in early mornings before anyone else awakens. I consider my office a reasonable setting for casual conservation and answering the telephone, but it is no place for thinking, writing, or worthwhile dialogue. Some colleagues have solved this by having two offices, one well-marked and located in the main corridor and intended for meeting other people, and the other for serious work, hidden away without clear identification. Flexibility does not preclude private work spaces. Ideally it provides the opportunity for those employees who want privacy to have it. A soft building does not, as a hard building would do, define everyone's job in terms of a private office, a shared office, or bull pen, and set this social order in concrete.

Small traditional societies can rely on accepted building types about which there is a clear consensus. In such societies everyone knows what a smoke house, a temple, or community building should look like. These forms are developed to fit the climate, topography, and the culture of a people. In the United States there is no clear consensus as to what a school should look like, much less what education should be. There is a strong movement in the service professions to de-emphasize large buildings to which clients come and instead bring the services out into the community. Western bureaucracy has always been subject to the twin pulls of centralization and decentralization. This dynamic tension between headquarters and branch offices is a creative force for institutional change. Bureaucrats and experts prefer talking among themselves to conversing with lay people. In time the central office becomes too large, unwieldy, expensive, and too remote from the

---

[1] John Boice, *Evaluation: Two Studies of SCSD Schools*. Research Report No. 2, distributed by Building Systems Information Clearinghouse, 3000 Sand Hill Road, Menlo Park, Ca. 94025.

branches to manage properly and the move toward decentralization begins, setting in motion another phase of the cycle.

Without a consensus as to the size and type of institutions, there can be no agreement on the physical form or size of buildings. Often a consensus is assumed that reflects only the interests of a small segment of the people affected. The influence of custodians and maintenance personnel in public buildings is often excessive. Furniture layouts which in theory are flexible become pseudo-fixed. The key to effective control over the environment is awareness on the part of the people affected. It is a mistaken belief that a building can educate people by itself. Without the physical presence of a teacher or therapist, learning is likely to be vague, unfocused, and centered about a single emotion. A building can have overall connotations of strength or warmth, but this is only educational in a very crude sense. Even this possibility of teaching design through metaphor will be lost if people detach themselves emotionally from their surroundings, tune out the buildings in which they live and work. There is ample evidence that this spatial numbness is present to an alarming degree. Most people feel no connection to the buildings in which they spend their working days. By default as well as design, this has produced even more hard and unresponsive buildings.

Airport furnishings represent a good illustration of the way that the interests of consumers (air travelers) have been neglected for the convenience of custodians and concessionaires. Air passengers, except for the elite using the private clubs subsidized by the economy passengers, have been putting up with sterile and sociofugal waiting areas for years. Flying isn't as much fun as it used to be and there isn't as much conversation as there might be, but it isn't easy to weigh this against the interests of custodians and concessionaires. The fact that people can adapt to cold and hard buildings has as much relevance to airport design as the finding that aquanauts can live under the sea. The question is not whether people can live this way, but whether they want to.

Anyone interested in changing society through a more humane environment must deal with the question of California malaise asked by Peter Schrag: "If it is so beautiful outside, why do I feel so bad?" [2]

[2] "How the West Was Lost," *World,* June 5, 1973, p. 28.

The question assumes a false distinction between the natural and the human environment. The California "outside" also includes tacky subdivisions, crowded freeways, the smog and earthquakes, as well as poverty, racism, and unemployment. Nor is there any evidence that Californians are more neurotic than residents of New York or Georgia. Virtually all of the crazy people I have met in California were raised elsewhere. (Frank Lloyd Wright said that the United States is tilted westwards, and everything loose falls into Southern California.) The benign climate also makes it possible to bring things out in the open that would be kept indoors in a harsher climate. The larger issue is that a beautiful climate does not by itself produce beautiful people. It does indeed *attract* people who want a beautiful climate, but if these happen to be numerous, the result will be crowding and its attendant problems. Good housing won't by itself cure the neuroses of the people who come to California, but it will make life better for those who remain. To the question about outward beauty and inner pain, one can only answer, "If it weren't so nice, you would feel worse, and if the contrast between natural landscape the human landscape is so stressful, you might consider moving to a place where you can be totally depressed."

Two objections to the idea of softening hard buildings are that this approach doesn't go far enough and it puts the cart before the horse. Let me deal with these criticisms in turn. I am sympathetic to demands for sweeping reforms and radical transformations provided the speaker knows what he is talking about. The prison system in this country is in trouble, but so are the schools, the churches, the family, and almost every other social institution. Ferment is part of the dynamic adaptiveness of institutions in a democratic society. Most of these problems are chronic rather than acute. When they reach crisis proportions—when prisoners riot or tenants hold back rent—some immediate short-term ameliorative action will be taken. The squeaky wheel gets the grease and sometimes a shiny new hubcap instead of a major overhaul. However, there is no inherent contradiction between minor and major changes, between small improvements and radical transformations. I use the word "inherent" because sometimes people can be bought off through token actions or name changes when they should be insisting upon major improvements. The critical factor is whether or not the minor changes are made in the spirit of improving the overall situation or to keep people quiet. In the labyrinthine maze of a school, hospital, or housing project, it is difficult enough to accomplish small changes, but it is from these modest indigenous efforts that people draw strength and vision toward larger and more fundamental changes. There is an old Presbyterian hymn that begins "Brighten Up the Corner Where You Live." Even though such efforts can be considered cosmetology, they also perform a valuable educational function.

In the natural world, the most common way an organism deals with a noxious situation is physical withdrawal. In urban society people cannot avoid pathogenic conditions such as noise, smog, ugliness, congestion, and brutality. The insult is so encompassing that paralysis and psychological withdrawal substitute for physical avoidance. Giving people small tangible goals which they can realize within the context of their own lives seems the best prescription for change. Painting murals on windowless walls or growing morning glories on the wire fence surrounding the asphalt yard is not going to transform a school but these are steps in the right direction because they reveal that people can affect their environment. Such efforts at humanizing space will also compel people to pay attention. This is one reason why such small-scale efforts are likely to be resisted by those who would encourage apathy and individual isolation in the interests of internal security. The warden who runs a tight prison or the principal who runs a tight school prefers people to be isolated and apathetic. Responding to nothing within themselves, inmates will follow orders. I am less impressed with the educational value of repeated failure which usually leads to withdrawal and rationalization than with the innervating effects of small successes that result in tangible improvements in a person's life situation for which he can take some personal responsibility.

This would surely be a humane world if every man, woman, and child acted humanely, but this is pure tautology. A view of people apart from the physical and cultural environment is as limited as an architect's view of buildings without people. We are the caretakers of this small and insignificant bit of the solar system; interdependency rules out architectural or psychological fundamentalism. The employee who bikes to work and uses his assigned parking space for flower boxes is not going to impress the fundamentalist. And as things are now, his superiors will probably look upon his actions as a highly subversive act (a threat to private property and the sanctity of the automobile) and take steps to remove the flower boxes and/or the employee.

A second objection to the idea of softening hard buildings is that it puts the cart before the horse. The argument is that the environment is a shambles because people's lives are a shambles; rather than trying to humanize society through softer buildings, we should start in the reverse direction. Once society is humanized, buildings will inevitably become more humane. This position is based on a limited model of causality. In the natural world, all effects influence their own causes. Once buildings are erected, they weave their own spell on occupants as well as on the people who planned them originally. Much has been written about alienated people, very little about the physical conditions which increase and maintain this alienation. Since the time of Freud, there has been a tendency to psychologize problems. A man's neurosis is a result of his mother's neurosis, and her problems are obviously a result of her mother's neurosis, and so on. The only way out of this tautology is to look at the conditions that produce and maintain neurosis.

Nothing is going to be done about hard buildings until people start tuning them in instead of tuning them out. Like the military parade complete with missile displays and jet aircraft flying overhead, a hard building cows occupants with its solidity, strength, and seeming permanence. It is easy for an outsider to criticize and offer suggestions for change, but much more difficult to work for it. In the 1950s, there was a vigorous campaign to reform mental hospitals. This was part of a large-scale effort to change a failing institution, which succeeded to the point where the large isolated mental hospitals followed the large orphanages into extinction. The same fate is in store for the large prison for the same reasons—the size, scale, and isolation make its efforts ineffectual. The suggestions offered for softening buildings are within the scope of the occupants themselves. External criticism, when it is not linked to specific recommendations within the context of people's lives, is likely to worsen an already bad situation and bore the outside public. There is a time for raising consciousness and a time for work to improve things.

Without a motive to come together or work together, people will find that hard and unresponsive buildings will increase their isolation. On the other hand, a shared task or external crisis can bring people together in even the hardest building. There was a great amount of community spirit and mutual assistance in the underground air raid shelters in Great Britain in World War II. These were people who had something in common—specifically, a desire to survive and a common enemy. Numerous research studies have showed that a common *external* enemy is the most effective means of uniting people.[3] Yet it also is clear that shared tasks and a common purpose (other than resisting an external enemy) can also unite people. The question of whether a common enemy cements a stronger bond than a shared task must also consider the undesirable consequences of external conflicts and wars. The destructive potential of today's weapons and the range of delivery system is so great, the interdependency of all life on the planet so evident, that the risks are too high in relying on external enemies to unite people.

An intense effort to achieve a common goal can succeed at least temporarily in humanizing even the hardest building. The basement of the architecture building at Berkeley, one of the most unfriendly monumental buildings in which I have ever taught, proved to be a very exciting place during the protest demonstrations against the Cambodian invasion. It became the home of the Guerilla Graphics Group, who produced posters for the entire San Francisco Bay Area and coordinated all demonstrations and protest activities. It became "action central" for clusters of enthusiastic and committed young people. After the protests subsided, the basement returned to being an empty and unfriendly cavern. However I would not recommend a foreign invasion every year in order to bring people together to protest.

A high-rise dormitory on my own campus had also been a very isolated and unfriendly place. Students did not know one another or even bother to put their names on the doors. The lounges on each floor were rarely used and there were no common activities for the residents. All this changed when an experimental program for freshmen was housed in the building. All the occupants were registered in a single course, in addition to several other courses of each student's own choosing. The discussion sections for the common course were held in the dormitory lounges and led by the dorm advisors who also lived there. The residents had something in common and the dormitory became a very friendly place. People smiled at one another as they walked down the halls, posters and murals went up in the corridors, and morale improved dramatically.

[3] Muzafer Sherif and Carolyn W. Sherif, *Groups in Harmony and Tension* (New York: Harper, 1953).

These examples should make it clear that hard buildings will not isolate people who *want* to come together. The most insidious effects of sociofugal buildings will be upon people who lack the desire to come together. This situation typifies the college classroom or university office building where the rewards system for both student and faculty is based on individual achievement. There is no incentive for conversing with others or working with them. In some courses where competition is keen, students will not share lecture notes or examination preparation lest they improve their neighbor's chances for getting a good grade. People in this kind of situation will be most affected by a hard and unresponsive building.

A building can make a good situation better or a bad situation worse. Architectural layout is one factor among many that affects communication and morale. A great artist may be able to paint masterpieces in an unheated attic and a great poet can compose poems in a tiny and uncomfortable basement room. However one should not be in the position of designing buildings for heroes to triumph in spite of. Rather one should be designing buildings in which people of varying ability can carry out their daily tasks.

The fact that everything is connected with everything else has brought some people to the conclusion that any single change will be insufficient—everything will have to be changed at once or the effort will be wasted. This overwhelming insight produced either paralysis or the romantic dream of total change overnight. Yet the same concept of interdependency has a hopeful side. If everything is connected, a change in any part of the system will affect every other part. It is not illogical to attempt to humanize society by softening the local post office. If one is in fact the local postmaster, this is probably the most logical starting place. If one does not attempt to humanize spaces over which one exercises some control, it seems irresponsible to venture into a larger arena. In this complex and changing society there is no point in talking about the sequence of horses and carts. There are many ways to haul a load, many sequences for social change. All problems cannot be solved through the existence of humane buildings, but it is a beginning—and for the designers and managers of spaces it is a logical beginning.

INDEX